Learning Styles:
Implications for Improving Educational Practices

by Charles S. Claxton and Patricia H. Murrell

ASHE-ERIC Higher Education Report No. 4, 1987

Prepared by

Clearinghouse on Higher Education
The George Washington University

Published by

Association for the Study of
Higher Education

Jonathan D. Fife,
Series Editor

Cite as
Claxton, Charles S. and Murrell, Patricia H. *Learning Styles: Implications for Improving Education Practices.* ASHE-ERIC Higher Education Report No. 4. Washington, D.C.: Association for the Study of Higher Education, 1987.

Managing Editor: Christopher Rigaux
Manuscript Editor: Barbara M. Fishel/Editech

The ERIC Clearinghouse on Higher Education invites individuals to submit proposals for writing monographs for the Higher Education Report series. Proposals must include:
1. A detailed manuscript proposal of not more than five pages.
2. A chapter-by-chapter outline.
3. A 75-word summary to be used by several review committees for the initial screening and rating of each proposal.
4. A vita.
5. A writing sample.

Library of Congress Catalog Card Number 88-70151
ISSN 0884-0040
ISBN 0-913317-39–X

Cover design by Michael David Brown, Rockville, Maryland

ERIC **Clearinghouse on Higher Education**
School of Education and Human Development
The George Washington University
One Dupont Circle, Suite 630
Washington, D.C. 20036-1183

ASHE **Association for the Study of Higher Education**
Texas A&M University
Department of Educational Administration
Harrington Education Center
College Station, Texas 77843

This publication was prepared partially with funding from the Office of Educational Research and Improvement, U.S. Department of Education, under contract no. 400-86-0017. The opinions expressed in this report do not necessarily reflect the positions or policies of OERI or the Department.

EXECUTIVE SUMMARY

Teaching and learning practices in higher education urgently need improvement—witness the recommendations of several national commissions on higher education and the difficulties faculty face with the diverse preparation of today's students. Learning style is a concept that can be important in this movement, not only in informing teaching practices but also in bringing to the surface issues that help faculty and administrators think more deeply about their roles and the organizational culture in which they carry out their responsibilities.

Learning style has been the focus of considerable study, and a number of colleges and universities have made it an important part of their work. The many approaches to learning style can be examined at four levels: (1) personality, (2) information processing, (3) social interaction, and (4) instructional methods. One researcher, however, speculates that several models in fact describe correlates of two fundamental orientations in learning: "splitters," who tend to analyze information logically and break it down into smaller parts, and "lumpers," who tend to watch for patterns and relationships between the parts (Kirby 1979).

How Has Information about Learning Style Proven Useful in Improving Students' Learning?

Information about style can help faculty become more sensitive to the differences students bring to the classroom. It can also serve as a guide in designing learning experiences that match or mismatch students' styles, depending on the teacher's purpose. Matching is particularly appropriate in working with poorly prepared students and with new college students, as the most attrition occurs in these situations. Some studies show that identifying a student's style and then providing instruction consistent with that style contribute to more effective learning.

In other instances, some mismatching may be appropriate so that students' experiences help them to learn in new ways and to bring into play ways of thinking and aspects of the self not previously developed. Any mismatching, however, should be done with sensitivity and consideration for students, because the experience of discontinuity can be very threatening, particularly when students are weak in these areas. Knowledge of learning style can thus help faculty design experiences appropriate for students in terms of matching or mismatching and enable them to do so thoughtfully and systematically.

Although some students bring a very instrumental orientation to learning, it may say more about their developmental stage than about learning style. The relationship between the two is not fully clear, and future major research will develop a better understanding in this area.

Some evidence suggests that students can expand their repertoire of learning strategies. Helping them understand more about their own preferences for learning and suggesting ways to cope more effectively in courses taught in ways inconsistent with their style are promising strategies. Doing so can also help students take increasing charge of their own learning and to be more active in the process. Learning how to learn is thus an empowering experience that students need if they are to be successful lifelong learners.

How Can Information about Learning Style Be Used outside the Classroom?
Information about learning style is extremely helpful in student affairs. In counseling, for example, style may suggest which approaches to counseling to use for particular students. Further, when students have problems in courses, it can guide counselors' efforts at intervention. In orientation, it can help students understand their own preferences and strengths in learning and be a stimulus for developing new ways of learning.

Learning style is useful in the work setting as well. It enables administrative leaders to be more insightful about using staff members in ways that call on their greatest strengths—a particularly important feature in the future as colleges and universities focus more on individuals' ability to perform tasks than on where they are in the organizational hierarchy. At the same time, the use of information about learning styles reminds us that an institution that is seriously interested in the development of students as a purpose needs to embrace such a concept for faculty and administrators as well.

Anecdotal information describes how some colleges have succeeded in institutionalizing the use of learning style. The most successful uses seem to occur when substantial faculty development activities raise people's consciousness about individual differences, when faculty develop some insight into how they themselves learn, when resources for helping faculty use information about learning styles are in place, when faculty and student affairs personnel work together to develop curricular responses to diverse learning styles, and when credit courses or orientation activities focus on helping students learn about their

own preferences for learning and on developing strategies for
learning in new ways.

Where Is Additional Research Needed?
The most pressing need is to learn more about the learning
styles of minority students—a particularly important subject in
the face of participation and graduation rates that indicate
higher education is not serving black students well. Changing
demographics portend an even more diverse student body
in the future, with increasing numbers of Hispanics and other
ethnic groups. Instruments that take cultural differences
into account need to be developed.

Second, research is needed to clarify how much difference it
makes if teaching methods are incongruent with a student's
style. Studies that speak to the role and potency of style, seen
in conjunction with other important variables, would help
teachers significantly. The development of better instrumentation to identify styles should be a key part of such research.

Third, research is needed to illuminate the connections and
interaction between style, developmental stage, disciplinary
perspectives, and epistemology. A better understanding of the
links between them would provide a helpful framework for examining teaching methodologies, the role of learning in individual development, and the use of the disciplines to promote
more complex and integrative thinking.

**Is Learning Style Connected to the Need for
Greater Collaboration and a Sense of Community in
Colleges and Universities?**
The Carnegie Foundation for the Advancement of Teaching has
said that much of higher education offers several striking
paradoxes. In particular, many faculty members report that
they work in highly individualistic and competitive ways and
yet yearn for a greater sense of community in their work. And
most efforts at building community, such as the creation of interdisciplinary courses and the use of team teaching, do not
really get to the core of the problem. The issues that must be
addressed are at the epistemological level, that is, in our very
ways of knowing, and every way of knowing becomes its own
ethic and thus a way of experiencing and shaping the world.
Presently the dominant epistemology, objectivism, with its emphasis on detachment and analysis, is anticommunal (Palmer
1987). An alternative, more intuitive, and more subjective way

of knowing needs to be honored as well, and it must be used in creative tension alongside objectivism if colleges and universities are serious about building community. Thus, teaching practices that honor both objectivist and relational ways of knowing may be considered the hallmarks of institutions genuinely committed to human development as an overarching purpose.

What Steps Should Institutions Take to Promote More Effective Learning through the Use of Learning Style?
1. *Conduct professional development activities on the use of learning style in improving teaching and student development functions.*

Professional development should go beyond traditional practices like sabbaticals and travel to professional meetings, as important as they are. Workshops, the use of minigrants for instructional improvement projects, seminars, and other functions can be very useful in helping the participants understand the importance of style.

2. *Promote the concept of classroom research and make data about learning style an integral part of it.*

Classroom research is an important strategy in achieving a greater balance in the way many institutions prize research and undervalue teaching, and the definition of research should be broadened to include not only research in the specialized disciplines but also in teaching-learning processes related to teaching in the disciplines (Cross 1987). Information about style, when linked with other data about students, holds great promise for helping faculty members to improve their teaching. The collection and use of such data, done formally or informally, can also contribute to a continuing dialogue among faculty and administrators as they learn from each other about teaching and learning.

3. *Establish curricular experiences that focus on helping students learn how to learn.*

Orientation activities or a credit course called "An Introduction to College" can be geared toward helping students gain a greater understanding of how learning occurs and their responsibility in the process. Inventories of learning style and other processes can be used to help make students aware of their own preferences and strengths. Attention should also be given to helping them develop strategies for succeeding in courses taught in ways that are incongruent with their primary learning abilities.

4. *In hiring new faculty members, take into account candidates' understanding of teaching-learning practices that recognize individual differences, including learning style.*

In the next 10 to 20 years, colleges and universities will hire thousands of new faculty members. In the past, the Ph.D., with its emphasis on specialized study in the discipline and its predominant orientation to research, was taken as the necessary credential for teaching, but today, with an increasingly diverse student body and research that clearly identifies the elements of effective college teaching (Cross 1987), administrators are coming to a greater realization that faculty preparation should include other areas of knowledge as well. Research in student development, learning theory, and ways to use the creative tension between content and process are all important prerequisites for effective teaching. Administrators have the opportunity to make a major contribution to improved learning by hiring faculty who have such preparation.

ADVISORY BOARD

Roger G. Baldwin
Assistant Professor of Education
College of William and Mary

Carol M. Boyer
Senior Policy Analyst for Higher Education
Education Commission of the States

Clifton F. Conrad
Professor of Higher Education
Department of Educational Administration
University of Wisconsin–Madison

Elaine H. El-Khawas
Vice President
Policy Analysis and Research
American Council on Education

Martin Finkelstein
Associate Professor of Higher Education Administration
Seton Hall University

Carol Everly Floyd
Associate Vice Chancellor for Academic Affairs
Board of Regents of the Regency Universities System
State of Illinois

George D. Kuh
Associate Dean for Academic Affairs
School of Education
Indiana University

Yvonna S. Lincoln
Associate Professor of Higher Education
University of Kansas

Richard F. Wilson
Assistant to the Chancellor
University of Illinois

Ami Zusman
Principal Analyst, Academic Affairs
University of California

CONSULTING EDITORS

Paul A. Albrecht
Executive Vice President and Dean
Claremont Graduate School

Harriet W. Cabell
Associate Dean for Adult Education
Director, External Degree Program
University of Alabama

L. Leon Campbell
Provost and Vice President for Academic Affairs
University of Delaware

Roderick S. French
Vice President for Academic Affairs
George Washington University

Timothy Gallineau
Vice President for Student Development
Saint Bonaventure University

Milton Greenberg
Provost
American University

Margaret Heim
Senior Research Officer
Teachers Insurance and Annuity Association/College
  Retirement Equity Fund

Frederic Jacobs
Dean of the Faculties
American University

Hans H. Jenny
Executive Vice President
Chapman College

Joseph Katz
Director, New Jersey Master Faculty Program
Woodrow Wilson National Fellowship Foundation

L. Lee Knefelkamp
Dean, School of Education
American University

David A. Kolb
Professor and Chairman
Department of Organizational Behavior
The Weatherhead School of Management
Case Western Reserve University

Jules B. LaPidus
President
Council of Graduate Schools in the United States

Judith B. McLaughlin
Research Associate on Education and Sociology
Harvard University

Theodore J. Marchese
Vice President
American Association for Higher Education

John D. Marshall
Assistant to the Executive Vice President and Provost
Georgia State University

Sheila A. Murdick
Director, National Program on Noncollegiate-Sponsored
 Instruction
New York State Board of Regents

Steven G. Olswang
Assistant Provost for Academic Affairs
University of Washington

Thomas J. Quatroche
Professor and Chair, Educational Foundations Department
State University College at Buffalo

S. Andrew Schaffer
Vice President and General Counsel
New York University

Henry A. Spille
Director, Office on Educational Credits and Credentials
American Council on Education

CONTENTS

FOREWORD

Accountability, assessment, value-added—no matter which
buzz word one chooses, it still indicates society's increasing
concern for quality higher education. Anything an institution
can do to improve its teaching process will benefit quality and
effectiveness. A frequently overlooked but somewhat obvious
consideration is that student learning styles differ. An awareness of this difference will help maximize the overall learning
process.

As described by Charles Claxton, associate professor, and
Patricia Murrell, professor, both of the Center for the Study of
Higher Education at Memphis State University, studies of
learning styles have concentrated on four areas: character traits,
reasoning ability, classroom contact, and teaching techniques.
Although each can influence the student, the instructor may be
unable to affect some elements. The authors offer a clear analysis of the four models, examples of their uses, and some
caveats.

Is it possible for institutions, large or small, to implement
procedures that can accommodate different learning styles? The
answer is unequivocally Yes! But it cannot be done haphaz-
ardly and be successful. Faculty commitment is the obvious
key element for the success of any program in developing and
enhancing sensitivity to learning styles. Instructors tend to use
various teaching methods based on their own personal experiences and what they found pleasing rather than on how knowledge is actually acquired. Studying learning styles can help correct this deficiency. Claxton and Murrell review these issues
and then identify steps that institutions can take to enhance the
learning process. Steps include publicizing classroom research
findings, offering specific workshops, and sharing information
about learning styles with students.

Through these steps, not only can an institution gain higher
efficiency and quality in its academic endeavors, but it will become more sensitive to the general learning process. Such efforts can only serve to enhance an institution's reputation or
stature.

Jonathan D. Fife
Professor and Director
ERIC Clearinghouse on Higher Education
School of Education and Human Development
The George Washington University

ACKNOWLEDGMENTS

We wish to express our appreciation to Sue Peterson, doctoral student in the Center for the Study of Higher Education at Memphis State University. We are grateful to her not only for her remarkable energy in assisting us with the research but also for her insight and commitment to student development.

CONTEXT

The concept of learning style has both promise and problems associated with it. While some researchers believe that "style is the most important concept to demand attention in education in many years [and] is at the core of what it means to be a person" (Guild and Garger 1985, p. viii), other commentators believe that researchers "have not yet unequivocally established the reality or utility of [the] concept" (Curry 1983, p. 6).

Learning style draws the attention of faculty and administrators in higher education in an almost compelling way. The sense that individual faculty members have of how they learn, their awareness that others often seem to approach things differently, and their successes and failures with different groups (even when those groups are taught the same way) reveal clearly that students learn differently. Except for some relatively isolated situations and the work of particular individuals, however, it is fair to say that learning style has not significantly affected educational practices in higher education for a number of reasons. The academy's emphasis on research in the traditional disciplines where the study of teaching and learning is not a major concern is one reason. But part of the reason is that different writers use the word "style" to mean many different things. Furthermore, the issues surrounding the concept are often poorly framed and the characteristics of learners associated with it difficult to assess.

Yet the need to improve educational practices is great, particularly in light of today's diversely prepared students and the current emphasis on effective teaching (Cross 1986) and assessment of outcomes (Education Commission of the States 1986). Learning style can be an extremely important element in the move to improve curricula and teaching in higher education.

The concept is important not so much in and of itself, but because it is one of several critical variables that faculty and other professionals can use in dealing with the complex issues of teaching and learning. Consideration of styles is one way to help faculty and administrators think more deeply about their roles and the organizational culture in which they carry out their work. A major research report on learning (Marton, Hounsell, and Entwistle 1984) reveals:

> ...an evolution in conceptualization and methodology that is informative beyond the findings. The more the researchers have realized the implications of different students' approaches to a page of text, for example, the more they have

Learning style draws the attention of faculty and administrators in higher education in an almost compelling way.

even though there's confusion about learning styles

broadened their concepts and terms. They write, in some hu-
mility, of their realization that they are. . .looking at issues
vital in education generally, in teaching, assessment, and
ethos [and that]. . .good teaching is. . .derivative,. . .born
not of its own rules but of those governing the process it
serves (Perry 1986, p. 187).

This suggestion that development of the person should be the
central purpose of education is one that guides the discussion in
this monograph, which looks at several models of learning style
and research on their use in college teaching, in student affairs,
and in the work setting and relates learning style to other
key issues in today's higher education. The links between the
recent substantial body of literature on human development and
learning style provide not only a source of practical suggestions
for college administrators but also a way of thinking about institutional purpose and effective educational practices.

HISTORICAL DEVELOPMENT

That people learn differently is certainly not a new idea (Fizzell 1984). Many inventories of learning style lead to conclusions that were formulated over 2,500 years ago. "At that time, people were seen as active or passive and as emotional or thoughtful. From these elements, the ancient Hindus proposed that peopled needed four basic ways of practicing religion—the four yogas or pathways—which are described in the Bhagavad Gita." The similarity of these ancient findings to those of today "must be more than chance" (p. 304).

Several strands in the evolution of the study of style have been identified (Guild and Garger 1985, pp. 11–14). Psychologists in Germany were considering cognitive style around 1900; Carl Jung's work on "psychological types" first appeared in 1921. Gordon Allport used the word "style" to refer to consistent patterns on the part of individuals. Lowenfield identified "haptic types," who experienced the world primarily through touch, and "visual types," who relied on seeing. Klein (1951) identified "levelers," who tended to retreat from objects and avoid competition, and "sharpeners," who tended to be competitive and had a great need for attainment and autonomy.

An incident from two centuries ago illustrates a problem caused by the incongruence between teacher and learner, an important part of the evolution of learning style as an object of study. At Greenwich Observatory in 1796:

> *The astronomer Maskelyn fired his assistant Kinnebrook for calibrating the clock incorrectly—or, at least, for not calibrating it exactly as Maskelyn did. Although Kinnebrook had been given a few months to improve his skill, he apparently got worse instead of better and was dismissed. . . .The error was serious for two reasons. The clock at Greenwich was used as a standard for all other observatories, and as every employee since has discovered, persistent disagreeing with one's boss is not wise* (Grasha 1984, p. 46).

Some 20 years later, another astronomer, Bessel, read about the dismissal and began investigating whether workers performed consistently when calibrating clocks, according to Edware Boring, author of a history of experimental psychology. Bessel found that the workers calibrated the clock differently and developed a formula to help astronomers correct for the lack of consistency in the way clocks were calibrated. "Boring suggests that this was the first attempt to study individual differences objectively and to use the information to improve the quality of life" (Grasha 1984, p. 46). Since then, researchers have examined all sorts of human characteristics in an effort to understand and to be able to predict behavior. "Somewhere in all of this, and I am uncertain about whether it represents a part of the mainstream journey or an interesting side trip, is the study of learning styles. Their study has evolved from the historical interest in individual differences" (p. 46).

Despite seminal research on individual differences by Allport (1961) and others in the 1940s and 1950s, interest in the types declined thereafter. Tyler believed interest waned because tests of students' perceptual sensitivities showed little relationship to achievement in school, while test results on intellectual characteristics were found to be highly predictive. "Whereas it was 'better' to have a high IQ rather than a low IQ, it could not be proven that it was better to have a certain perceptual sensitivity. In terms of school success, style by itself was neutral" (Guild and Garger 1985, p. 13).

Research by E.L. Thorndike in the early 1900s indicated that a student's achievement was highly correlated with intelligence, a seemingly logical finding that has profoundly influenced educators' thinking about learning ever since (Henson and Borthwick 1984). Yet "the conditions set for these studies were such that all students were given the same type of instruction and the same amount of time to learn" (p.4). In 1963, John B. Carroll reported the results of his experiment in which he used a variety of teaching approaches and students were able to have as much time as they needed. "Under these conditions the findings were totally different. Students aptitude proved not to be a major factor in determining achievement" (p. 4).

The implications of such findings are extraordinary. "They can be interpreted to mean that given the needed time and the correct teaching methods, almost any students can learn or master the material set before them" (Henson and Borthwick 1984, p. 4). The research of Benjamin Bloom and others furthered this work, giving rise to the concept of mastery learning, in which students' achievement is held constant and teaching methods, materials, and time available are sufficiently flexible so that practically all learners are able to achieve at a high level. Clearly contained within this approach is a recognition "that individual learners have their own preferred learning styles and that teachers have some responsibility for gearing up their teaching style to "fit" the preferred learning style of the learners" (p. 4).

Even though research about learning style as an important aspect of individual differences has not proceeded as rapidly as one might have hoped, the emphasis of psychologists in the 1960s and 1970s was more on differences between groups (Curry 1983), including differences in race, sex, and social class. This decreased interest in research on learning style was "unfortunately premature and left the whole field of investigation fragmented and incomplete" (p. 2).

The relative lack of focus can be seen in the absence of a clear definition of learning style and the contradictory research results, perhaps because learning style has been addressed by researchers in various disciplines who were asking different questions and focusing on different aspects of the learning process (Hendricson, Berlocher, and Herbert 1987). "Educational psychologists, primarily in European schools of education, have focused on how students study and some of the more practical aspects of learning styles. In North America, work in the area of learning styles has been more theoretical in nature and researchers have generally approached the topic from the perspective of cognitive and psychomotor psychology" (p. 175).

One way to organize the several strands of research on learning styles and teaching is the metaphor of an onion, in which the layers of the onion are analogous to the different levels of a person's characteristics, which could be called "style" (see figure 1) (Curry 1983). At the core of the onion is style in the sense of basic characteristics of personality. Information-processing models, describing how persons tend to take in and process information, form the second layer; social-interaction models, dealing with how students tend to interact and behave in the classroom, make up the third; and learning environments and instructional preferences constitute the fourth.

The traits described at the different levels are not discrete, of course, and as one moves from the core level of personality to the fourth level of instructional preference, it is clear that the traits of each level influence the next. The traits at the core are the most stable and thus are the least subject to change in response to intervention by the researcher or instructor. As the levels proceed outward, the traits or preferences are less stable and more susceptible to change. In all likelihood, the volatility of tools for measuring these traits increases the farther removed the traits are from the core, helping to explain why it is increasingly difficult to develop valid and reliable measures to assess students' style that a teacher or researcher can address and resulting in some of teachers' frustration as they attempt to use research on style to enhance practices in the classroom.

FIGURE 1
A FRAMEWORK OF LEARNING STYLE MODELS

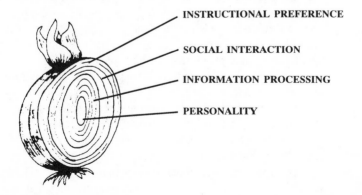

INSTRUCTIONAL PREFERENCE

SOCIAL INTERACTION

INFORMATION PROCESSING

PERSONALITY

Source: Adapted from Curry 1983.

Personality Models
Field dependence and independence
Herman A. Witkin, whose "work is the most extensive and in-depth research on cognitive style conducted in the last 50 years" (Guild and Garger 1985, p. xii), focused on the field dependence-independence dimension of cognitive style. His 1954 report, *Personality through Perception*, is the culmination of several years of research, primarily on field dependence-independence, but since its publication, a number of other researchers have added findings on this important dimension.

The tools used to study field dependence-independence are the rod-and-frame test, the body-adjustment test, and the embedded-figures test (Witkin 1976). In the rod-and-frame test, the subject is seated in a darkened room and shown a luminous rod situated in a luminous frame. The rod and frame can be adjusted independently, and the subject is asked to move the rod to the true vertical position as the frame is slanted. Some subjects adjust the rod to alignment with the frame (even when the frame is slanted to the left or to the right) and then say that the rod is upright. Other subjects adjust the rod to the upright position, irrespective of the tilt of the surrounding frame.

In the body-adjustment test, the subject is seated in a chair inside a small, specially constructed room, both of which can be moved independently. The subject is then asked to adjust his or her body to the upright position. Some people adjust the body to the surrounding tilted room and then report they are sitting in an upright position. Others adjust the body to an upright position independently of the angle of the room.

In the embedded-figures test, the subject is shown a simple figure, such as a square or rectangle, and then shows a more complex figure that has within it the first simple figure. The subject is then asked to find the simple figure within the complex figure. Some people easily locate the simple figure in the complex one, while others have difficulty or are unable to do so in the time allowed.

While the embedded-figures test does not involve space orientation, as the first two do, the task is essentially the same—to perceive the object accurately without being influenced by the surrounding field. People tend to be consistent in their performance on all three tests (Witkin 1976, p. 41). Persons who are heavily influenced by the surrounding field are called "field dependent"; those who are relatively uninfluenced by the surrounding field are called "field independent." At the outset, however, one must recognize that the world is not made up of two types of people—field dependents and field independents. Rather, a person's standing on this dimension is described by his or her position relative to the mean.

Field dependents and field independents differ not only in their perceptual ability in the laboratory but also in their social interaction.

> *The person who, in the laboratory, is strongly influenced by the surrounding visual framework in his perception of an item within it is also likely, in social situations, to use the prevailing social frame of reference to define his attitudes, his beliefs, his feelings, and even his self-view from moment to moment. Thus, if you substitute for the square wooden frame a social frame of reference, and for the rod, an attribute of the self, such as an attitude or sentiment, there is indeed continuity in what a person is likely to do in both laboratory perceptual situations and social situations* (Witkin 1976, p. 43).

What causes a person to be field dependent or field independent? Genetic factors are apparently very important although less so than socialization and child-rearing experiences. In appears that the early experiences children have with their mothers are important: Field-independent persons were encouraged at an early age to be autonomous. This finding has held in a number of cross-cultural studies of peoples as varied as Europeans, the Eskimos of Baffin Bay, and the Temme of Sierra Leone. Field dependents are more strongly influenced by authority figures and by peer groups that are field independents. Field dependents and field independents exhibit differences in speech patterns, field dependents referring more to others than to themselves as they talk, field independents using more personal pronouns and active verbs ("I did this" rather than "this happened to me") (Witkin 1976).

Studies in academic contexts have demonstrated that field dependence-independence is a significant variable in a student's selection of major, course, and career. Field-independent students clearly favor areas of study that call for analytic skills, such as mathematics, engineering, and science. Field-dependent students favor areas that call for more extensive interpersonal relations, such as social science, the humanities, counseling, teaching, and sales (Witkin 1976).

Studies in academic contexts have demonstrated that field dependence-independence is a significant variable in a student's selection of major, course, and career.

Among graduate students in psychology, the more field dependent chose clinical psychology, while the more field independent chose experimental psychology. Among high achievers in nursing, the more field-dependent students chose psychiatric nursing, the more field independent surgical nursing. Persons studying systems engineering were found to be more field independent that were engineers in other categories (Witkin 1976).

More women than men have been found to be field dependent. Women tend to choose work that calls for more interaction with others, while men select careers that call for analytic skills. Field-independent women tend to score at the masculine end of scales that measure masculinity/femininity. As male/female norms change as a result of changing sex roles in the American society, it will be interesting to see whether the sex differences found in the earlier studies hold (Witkin 1976).

A substantial body of research on elementary and secondary school teachers suggests that those in mathematics and science are more likely to be field independent, while social science teachers are more likely to be field dependent. Field-dependent teachers prefer discussion methods of teaching, while more field-independent teachers prefer the lecture method. Field-independent teachers tend to be more direct in attempting to influence students, while field-dependent teachers are more inclined to employ democratic procedures in the classroom (Witkin 1976).

When students and teachers were matched and mismatched in terms of field dependence and independence, the matched subjects described each other positively, and the mismatched subjects described each other negatively. When the teachers described their students' abilities, they valued more highly the attributes of students who were like themselves. Similarly, the students felt more positively about the teachers who were like themselves in terms of cognitive skills (Witkin 1976).

Does teaching in ways that match students' field-dependent or -independent style result in improved learning? The little existing research on that question is contradictory. A study of 64 undergraduates in a recreation education program at a Big 10 university explored the question of whether students categorized as field dependent and field independent would learn more with instruction oriented to their style (Macneil 1980). Using instructional style (a discovery approach and an expository approach) and cognitive style as independent variables and a "no treatment" control group, the researcher trained graduate-level instructors to teach classes that were equally divided between field-dependent and field-independent students randomly assigned to the sections. The assumption was that field dependents would learn more from the discovery approach and field independents from the expository method. Those results did not occur, however: Achievement did not vary as a function of style.

This finding was consistent with those of four other studies, all of which were of students in junior high and lower grades. Thus, "the field dependent and independent dimension of cognitive style may not be as fruitful an avenue for scientific investigation as some would suggest" (Mcneil 1980, p. 358).

Other research studied the interaction between level of guidance provided in a math class and field dependence or independence (Adams and McLeod 1979). Four sections of a course were designed for prospective elementary teachers; 83 percent were females and most were seniors. "Two levels of guidance, low and high, were chosen, varying the amount of structure, cue salience, and active involvement by the student. . . .The high guidance treatment. . .was designed as a compensatory treatment for field-independent students. . . .It was expected that field-independent students would do better using the low guidance material, whereas field-dependent students would do better using the high guidance materials" (pp. 348–49). The "expected interaction between field dependence/independence and achievement failed to occur," however (p. 354).

Thus, the study indicates, matching the instructional method and cognitive style and matching the degree of guidance and cognitive style and matching the degree of guidance and cognitive style did not lead to improved learning. A different study obtained different results, however (Abraham 1985). In a study of teaching English as a second language, data on 61 students from a variety of language backgrounds focused on whether a teaching approach that did not emphasize rules would be of greater benefit to field-dependent students, noting that earlier research had found "field-independent students are more adept at learning and using rules than field-dependent students" (p. 691). The researcher used two computer-assisted instruction lessons, one traditional, rule oriented, and deductive, the other providing many examples and deemphasizing rules. A paper-and-pencil test containing 20 pairs of sentences was used as a pretest and a post-test. As expected, the "field-independent student performed better with the deductive approach. . .Field-

dependent students performed better with the example lesson" (p. 699). The results, however, accounted for only a fourth of the variance among post-test scores; other factors, such as language background, motivation, and attitude, should also be considered.

The work of such researchers brings into focus the fact that matching can be addressed in several ways—students and teachers of the same style (Witkin 1976), instructional method and students' style (Abraham 1985; Macneil 1980), for example—but the research is contradictory as to which approach to matching offers the most payoff in terms of students' learning.

Does one teach the way one learns? Some research suggests that we do (Witkin 1976, p. 9), although it may not be the case for style as described by models at the other three levels of the framework. But if it is true, is it possible for a person of one style to learn to teach in another? For example, could a field-dependent teacher who tends to rely on discovery methods learn to be skillful and comfortable with more field-independent approaches, such as lectures? If the answer is "yes" and if it were clear that matching instructional style to students' style promoted more effective learning such matching would not only be possible but could also lead to more successful students in college. Researchers need to consider these two important issues.

A criticism of Witkin's model is its use of somewhat negative-sounding traits in field dependents. Further, as more women than men tend to be field dependent, some people view the description of this style as sexist. Ramirez and Castaneda (1974) use the term "field sensitive" rather than "field dependent," for example, concerned that Mexican-American children are penalized in Anglo schools, which are oriented more toward field-independent learners, while their own culture is oriented more toward field-sensitive qualities. Material they have developed can increase teachers' awareness that they may teach in ways that convey the message that field-independent thinking is superior to field-sensitive thinking. Ramirez and Castaneda encourage teachers to provide a balance of the two orientations, that is, "to teach bicognitively" (Kirby 1979, p. 86), as students clearly need to have skills in both.

The belief that Mexican-American children are more field sensitive may have important implications for effective college teaching in the coming years. "By around the year 2000, America will be a nation in which one of every three of us will be nonwhite" (Hodgkinson 1985, p. 7). Research that showed whether field-sensitive students would learn better when they are matched in terms of the teacher's style, the teaching method, or the level of structure could be very useful in designing classroom experiences. Further, the possibility of teachers' greater reliance on "field-sensitive methods," which might roughly be labeled such methods as class discussions, simulations, and work in small groups, is also in keeping with the current call for greater emphasis in the classroom on collaborative learning (Bruffee 1987).

The extensive body of research on field dependence and independence, however, has not significantly affected college teaching. For one thing, the research was not originally directed to teaching. Thus, the instrumentation, such as the embedded-figure test, does not provide results that can be easily translated into teaching practices. Further, if the results are interpreted to students, they may not gain much insight into their specific ways of learning because the model has only two dimensions.

At the same time, however, these two dimensions may be the two most fundamental ones. For example, the many different conceptions of style may be "only correlates of a few basic styles [that] fall under splitter and lumper types" (Kirby 1979, p. 36), "a distinction [that] overlaps 'left-brain' and 'right-brain' activity" (p. 4). Field independents may be in the splitter camp, field dependents in the lumper camp. Hence, this dimension may be a worthwhile avenue for research, not simply in terms of identifying the two styles but also as a more overarching construct that can illuminate the styles identified by other instruments and processes.

The Myers-Briggs Type Indicator

The Myers-Briggs Type Indicator (MBTI) is an instrument that was designed as an aid in applying Jungian theory in counseling, education, and business (Myers 1976). The essence of the theory is that seemingly random variations in behavior are actually consistent and orderly when one considers the different ways in which people prefer to take in information (their perception) and the ways in which they choose to make decisions (their judging function). Jung's theory states that the world can be perceived in two distinct ways—sensing or intuition—and that people use two distinct and contrasting ways to reach conclusions or make judgments—thinking or feeling (Myers and

Myers 1980). In addition to the person's preference on both of those mental functions is an accompanying preference for extraversion or introversion and a preference for the person's attitude toward life, which is either judging or perceptive.

The MBTI consists of four dichotomous scales: Extraversion versus Introversion (E-I), Sensing versus Intuition (S-N), Thinking versus Feeling (T-F), and Judging versus Perception (J-P). On the E-I scale, a person's preference for the direction of his or her energy and interest is either toward the outer world of persons, actions, and objects (E) or toward the inner world of ideas and concepts (I). On the S-N scale, a person's preference is either for perceiving the world through the realities of experience taken in by his or her five senses (S) or for perceiving the world by paying more attention to inferred meanings and possibilities (I). On the T-F scale, a person's preferences are determined by whether he or she relies more on logical order in making judgments (T) or more on personal values and importance (F). And on the J-P scale, the preferences are characterized by planning and controlling events (J) or by being flexible, waiting to see what happens, and reacting to events with spontaneity (P).

Extensive research conducted in the 1960s gave indirect evidence of differences in learning style by type (Lawrence 1984). In one study, Myers correlated the MBTI with the Edwards Personal Preference Schedule, where the results were consistent with the theory of type. Extraversion correlated moderately with dominance, sensing with order, thinking with endurance, judging with order, introversion with achievement, intuition with autonomy, feeling with nurturance, and perception with autonomy (Lawrence 1984). In another major study, the MBTI was correlated with the Personality Research Inventory, where perception is linked with tolerance of complexity as well as impulsiveness (Lawrence 1984). Extraversion correlated with talkativeness, sensing with gregariousness, judging with attitude toward work, and intuition with artistic qualities and liking to use the mind.

In a third study, faculty ratings of certain qualities of learning style were correlated with MBTI type. The findings, which have been replicated by others, concern the correlation of the judging function with qualities that help a person do well in college. Such qualities include thoroughness, responsibility, dependability, and the ability to meet deadlines, complete undertakings, and attend to details. The study also associated qualities like imagination, ability to analyze and deal with abstract concepts, and independence with intuitive types. It further linked such qualities as competitiveness, leadership, and expression of self with extroverts (Lawrence 1984).

Another researcher looked at performance of people of different types as it related to success in dealing with tasks of varying levels of complexity, linking the variable for extrovert and introvert with a measure of students' drive or anxiety level (Martray 1971). High-drive introverts and low-drive extroverts were found to be at a significant disadvantage in retaining complex verbal material. Extroverts were found to exhibit superior performance on simple or complex psychomotor tasks. And no differences were found in short- or long-term retention of simple verbal material.

Studies of types of students compared to types of instructors have found striking mismatches (Roberts 1977; Roberts and Lee 1977). A study of community colleges, for example, found that 63 percent of the teachers were intuitives, compared to only 26.5 percent of students (Roberts 1977), while a study of 77 upper-division students majoring in agricultural economics and 11 agricultural economics faculty members at Texas Tech University found that 78 percent of the students were sensing rather than intuitive, compared to only 55 percent of the teachers (Roberts and Lee 1977). Judging and perception were also mismatched: 82 percent of the teachers were judging, compared to only 42 percent of the students.

Intuitive types consistently score higher on aptitude measures based on reading and writing (McCaulley and Natter 1980, pp. 117–18), because they convert symbols into meaning, thus grasping concepts and ideas faster from written words and developing greater skills in reading. Sensing types have less natural interest in reading, take more time to read for details, and are "less motivated to learn to read unless they can see a practical use for reading" (p. 118). In studies of students at the Florida State University Developmental Reading School, intuitives significantly outscored sensing types on tests with theory and abstraction, while no significant difference occurred in their scores on computations or applications of principles (McCaulley and Natter 1980).

Research using the MBTI has also been found to be useful when the focus is on the teacher rather than on the student. The kinds of questions and the ways in which they were asked usually reflect the teacher's own preference for sensing or intuition

(Lawrence 1982). Sensing types ask questions that seek facts and details and to which responses are predictable. Intuitive questions call for synthesis and evaluation and usually invite imagining and hypothesizing. As a result, sensing teachers may neglect synthesizing and evaluation, while intuitive teachers may give little importance to facts and details (p. 81).

Teachers of different types are attracted to different levels and different subject matters (Lawrence 1982). Sensing teachers choose lower levels of education and are more likely to teach practical skills with facts and details, while intuitive teachers are more likely to be found in colleges and universities teaching courses rich in abstractions and theory. "In short, teachers tend to understand and appreciate students whose minds work like their own" (McCaulley and Natter 1980, pp. 185–86). Further, much available data support the hypothesis that intuitive types survive and thrive much better in an academic environment, particularly at the college level.

The MBTI is a very comprehensive instrument with high face validity.[1] Persons who take it typically say it describes their personality well. Faculty who are knowledgeable about type can generally develop suggestions on ways to orient their courses more to the students in their classes. Using the MBTI is an excellent way to foster a dialogue with students about how they learn. In the process, faculty can become more sensitive to the consequences of their match or mismatch with students in their classes.

Reflection versus impulsivity

The dimension of reflection versus impulsivity, the third model, is "the tendency [in problems with highly uncertain responses] to reflect over alternative solution possibilities, in contrast with the tendency to make an impulsive selection of a solution" (Kagan 1965, p. 609). The tests used to determine this tendency include the matching-figures test and the identical-pictures test. In the identical-pictures test, for example, the subject is to study a picture of an object (the standard), such as a geometric design, a house, or a car, and then is shown several similar stimuli, only one of which is identical to the standard. The subject's task is to select the picture that is the

[1]Because of the complexity of the instrument and the theory base, persons who wish to use it should have the approval of the Center for the Applications of Psychological Type in Gainesville, Florida.

same as the standard in a limited time. Impulsive subjects respond to this factor of conceptual tempo by glancing quickly at the sample and selecting the answer that appears most nearly correct. Reflective persons carefully examine each alternative before finally selecting what they believe is the correct one.

While a person's reflectivity or impulsivity is relatively stable over time (Kagan 1965), research has shown that a person's standing on this dimension can be changed. If an impulsive child is placed in a classroom with a reflective teacher, the child becomes more reflective (Nelson 1975). A study of 223 two-year and four-year college students found that on an identical-pictures test, *where* the correct choice appeared in the sequence of possible answers was important. When the correct answer was later in the sequence, the error rate quadrupled (p. 7).

The research on reflectivity versus impulsivity has important implications for improving college teaching.

The research on reflectivity versus impulsivity has important implications for improving college teaching. Heavy reliance on multiple-choice examinations may not give an accurate picture of how much a student actually knows, particularly for a student who feels under great pressure to achieve a certain grade, as pressure serves to intensify a person's tendency to be impulsive or reflective. Under these circumstances, it is very difficult for the impulsive person to take a more deliberate approach, and the reflective person can often become nearly immobilized and unable to finish a task.

The finding that a person's standing on this dimension can be changed somewhat is promising. Teachers could sensitize students to the fact that they can move too quickly (or too slowly) in answering questions on a test and urge them to be aware of that possibility.

Reliance on multiple-choice examinations occurs outside the classroom too, of course. Standardized examinations used in admitting students to undergraduate, graduate, and professional schools usually consist primarily of multiple-choice questions. They are also widely used in selecting candidates for jobs. Teachers, test developers, and employers should think seriously about developing evaluative tools that can gauge more accurately the level of knowledge people in fact possess.

Omnibus Personality Inventory
Another instrument that provides a comprehensive look at personality is the Omnibus Personality Inventory (OPI) developed in the late 1950s at the Center for Research and Develop-

ment in Higher Education at the University of California at Berkeley as a means of measuring the intellectual, interpersonal, and social-emotional development of college students. It consists of 14-scales that measure different modes of thinking, handling feelings and impulses, and ways of relating to self and others.

The instrument has been used to conduct longitudinal studies discriminating nine distinctive thinking-learning patterns (Katz and Henry *forthcoming*). Interestingly, these nine patterns relate to existing disciplines: scientific thinking, literary thinking, historical and philosophic thinking, thinking in the social sciences, thinking among artists, thinking in language and music, thinking among design engineers and architects, ideational thinking, and creative thinking. Using the OPI is helpful in that "once people become conscious about their distinctive cognitive style, they are able to learn better and to transcend limitations of their present ways of thinking" (p. 73). This comment makes an extremely important point about the value of style. Developmental theory (see Perry 1970 and Kegan 1982, for example) tells us that as people mature they move through predictable stages of thinking, each one more complex and more inclusive than the earlier ones. In early years, people are embedded in a more concrete, less self-reflective way of making meaning of the world, and a critical threshold of development is reached when a person begins to think about thinking. When faculty have insight into different learning styles—or, said another way, different ways of thinking—they are more able to help students become aware of their own thinking. Students are thereby helped to move to new ways of looking at themselves, their academic experiences, and the world (Katz and Henry *forthcoming*).

This work also points up the fact that learning style can be considered as a way of thinking and thus is linked to the disciplines, which are not only bodies of knowledge but also ways of thinking. Thus, style is an important element in the liberal arts core curriculum, where the objective for students is not just to learn content in the natural sciences, the humanities, and the social sciences. They can also be helped to develop skills in the ways of thinking that the different disciplines represent.

The Holland typology of personality
The Holland typology of personality posits six personality types:

1. *Realistic*. Persons who are interested in mechanical activities and in developing coordination and physical strength. They manipulate tools and other concrete objects and describe themselves as concrete, strong, and masculine rather than as socially skilled or sensitive.
2. *Investigative*. Persons who engage in thinking, organizing, and understanding. They involve themselves in scientific and scholarly activities and describe themselves as analytical, intellectual, curious, reserved, and scientific rather than as persuasive or social.
3. *Social*. Persons who find satisfaction in helping, teaching, and serving. They describe themselves as gregarious, friendly, cooperative, and tactful rather than as mechanical or technical.
4. *Conventional*. Persons who prefer orderly, structured situations with clear guidelines. They engage in clerical and computational activities and describe themselves as precise and accurate, clerical and conforming.
5. *Enterprising*. Persons who enjoy organizing, directing, or persuading other people and exercising authority. They describe themselves as persuasive, possessing leadership, ambitious, and optimistic.
6. *Artistic*. Persons who enjoy performing athletically or artistically. They describe themselves as emotional, aesthetic, autonomous, unconventional, impulsive, and imaginative (Holland 1966).

While the typology was originally developed for use in career development and to shed light on environmental preferences in the workplace, it is equally applicable in the classroom (Knefelkamp and Cornfeld 1979). Because a teaching method or a learning activity is an "environment," having faculty take the inventory can help them see that their use of particular teaching methodologies may be very appropriate for some students yet highly incongruent with the preferences of others. The results of the inventory do not immediately translate into particular teaching strategies; nevertheless, faculty members' awareness of students' preferences can sensitize them to the need for an array of learning activities rather than undue reliance on any one approach.

* * *

Research on field dependence and field independence tell us that matching can be done by matching students and teachers of the same style, matching instructional method and student style, and matching student style with the amount of structure provided by the teacher. The research is mixed, however, as to whether matching in any of these ways produces more effective learning, and additional study is clearly needed. Further research is needed as to whether teachers' own styles are such that they can learn to teach in ways other than their own and thus be responsive to the styles of their students.

Use of the term "field sensitive" can raise teachers' awareness of the need to honor field-sensitive thinking as well as field-independent thinking and to assist students in developing both.

The Myers-Briggs Type Indicator reveals a comprehensive portrait of the learner (and the teacher). Students do better or poorer on particular levels of learning tasks as a function of type. The strengths and orientations of faculty vary too as a function of type, and some evidence indicates a striking mismatch between faculty and students generally. Results of the MBTI can be extremely helpful in promoting dialogue among faculty and between faculty and students about their personality orientation and the implications for course design.

The dimension of reflectivity and impulsivity can help faculty think about the varied inclinations students have. In particular, tests should be scrutinized for bias against one style or the other. That the degree to which a person is impulsive or reflective can be changed somewhat points out that college courses can be designed not only to match students' styles but also to mismatch them in a judicious and considered way so as to help students enhance aspects of the self that are relatively undeveloped.

The Omnibus Personality Inventory can be used to help students become more aware of how they think, thereby facilitating their movement beyond limiting modes. The OPI has been a stimulus for the development of a framework of ways of thinking that meshes with the varied perspectives of the disciplines. It thus links style and the disciplines as ways of thinking or knowing.

Research on the Holland typology of personality indicates that people do prefer particular environments. A teaching methodology can be thought of as a classroom "environment," and thus faculty need to be sensitive to it and not limit learning activities to any one mode.

Overall, traits at this level are less susceptible to modification in response to changes in the environment or the instructor's actions. Thus, the major emphasis on research in the future may need to be determining how crucial matching or mismatching is and then designing learning activities consistent with those findings.

Information-Processing Models
The research of Pask

The second level of learning style models deals with the way people tend to process information. The research of Gordon Pask (1975, 1976) begins with a description of the learning strategies people use (Ford 1985). The first type, *holists*, use a global approach to learning and develop, early in the process, a broad framework of understanding into which they can then fit more detailed information. They typically look at several aspects of a topic at the same time, constantly make connections between the theoretical aspects and practical applications as they learn, and make substantial use of analogies. Holists study a subject from the "top down"; that is, they examine parts of the topic at the higher levels of complexity and make connections between them. Figure 2 depicts a typical holistic strategy. Each circle represents a particular aspect of the subject under consideration.

The second type, *serialists*, focus their attention more narrowly on pieces of information low in the hierarchical structure (see figure 3) and develop their understanding through logical, sequential, and well-defined steps. They use simple links to relate different aspects of the subject, thus working in a "bottom up" approach so that the overall picture is developed slowly, thoroughly, and logically. Theoretical and practical aspects are learned separately, rather like separate strands. Serialists use logical links rather than analogies to relate different parts of a subject. Pask's extensive research on matching and mismatching of material and types of learners shows that students learn faster and more effectively where a match occurs (Ford 1985, p. 120).

Further investigation has connected the concept of learning strategies to learning styles: Persons who use a holistic strategy are *comprehension learners*, and those who use a serialistic

FIGURE 2
HOLISTIC STRATEGY

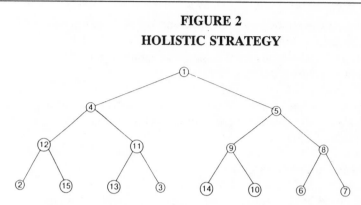

Note: Numbers relate to the sequence in which subtopics are learned.

Source: Ford 1985, p. 118.

FIGURE 3
SERIALISTIC STRATEGY

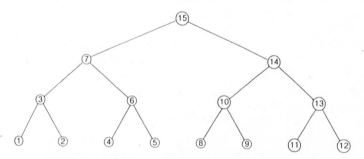

Note: Numbers relate to the sequence in which subtopics are learned.

Source: Ford 1985, p. 119.

strategy are *operation learners*. Pask calls these approaches learning styles, because the two strategies describe how a person approaches learning in general.

Two important components of understanding are *description building* and *procedure building*. The first is the building of a description or conceptual map of what is known about a particular topic, thus providing an overview of how topics are related. Procedure building, on the other hand, focuses on the evidence and procedures that undergird the broad overview. Developing the overall design of a house, for example, would be description building, while making the detailed plans for wiring and plumbing would be procedure building. Pask believes that both description building and procedure building are essential to the process of learning.

It is here that the critical link between learning style and learning outcome occurs. Pask believes that the global, holistic approach is the strongest vehicle for achieving description building. "Comprehension learners, with their global, holist bias, are better at description building than procedure building. Operation learners, with their local, serialist-like bias, are better at procedure building than description building" (Ford 1985, p. 120). Extreme comprehension learners may be quite skilled at building an overview but unable to give enough attention to the detailed evidence needed to support it. Thus, they may be subject to what Pask calls *"globetrotting,"* given to overgeneralizing without adequate evidence. Conversely, extreme operation learners may not have enough skill in description building, which Pask calls *"improvidence"* or "not being able to see the forest for the trees." Because both description building and procedure building are needed for full understanding, both approaches are needed in learning, and those who are skilled in both are called "versatile learners."

Siegel and Siegel

The issue of sequencing material is clearly related to learning style (McDade 1978). Ausubel (1963), for example, believes students learn more effectively if they are taught general, inclusive concepts first, which then act as an anchor for later details and examples ("subsumption"). In contrast, Siegel and Siegel (1965) describe a cognitive style that they term "educational set," a continuum "ranging from a preference to learn factually oriented material to preference to learn conceptually oriented material" (McDade 1978, p. 137). Ausubel believes learning concepts first is best for all learners, while the Siegels believe this sequence is best only for those learners whose educational sets are congruent with this subsumptive approach.

"A factually set learner prefers factual content for its own sake and is not motivated to interrelate the facts into a more complex framework. A conceptual set learner accepts facts as elements to be interrelated into a broader contextual whole, to learn principles, concepts, theories, and relationships" (McDade 1978, p. 137). A study of 90 students in an educational psychology course hypothesized that conceptually set students would learn better if they were taught in a subsumptive sequence, that is, concepts first and facts second, and in fact the results bore out the hypothesis. Conceptually set students performed better with the concepts-facts sequence, while factually set students performed better with the facts-concepts sequence when given a written examination.

Schmeck

In the third information-processing model, learning style is defined as "a predisposition on the part of some students to adopt a particular learning strategy regardless of the specific demands of the learning task. Thus, a style is simply a strategy that is used with some cross-situational consistency" (Schmeck 1983, p. 233). Closely related to style is learning strategy, which is "a pattern of information-processing activities used to prepare for an anticipated test of memory" (p. 234).

Two learning styles have been identified in terms of how people process information: "deep-elaborative" information processors or "shallow-reiterative" information processors (Schmeck 1981). "Deep processing involves devoting more attention to the meaning and classification of an idea suggested by a symbol than to the symbol itself " (p. 385). For example, in deep encoding a student would learn about "depression" by thinking about the fact that the word refers to an emotional state that is similar to other emotions in some ways and different in some others. In shallow encoding, a student would take note of how the word sounds and simply repeat it several times.

As processors of information, "students tend to be either habitually deep-elaborative. . .or shallow-reiterative" (Schmeck 1981, p. 384).

> *Deep-elaborative information processors spend more of their time thinking and less time repeating. They classify, contrast, analyze, and synthesize information from different sources. They elaborate by thinking of personal examples, visually imagining personal illustrations, and restating information in their own words. They draw upon the depth and breadth of their experiences* (Schmeck 1981, pp. 384–85).

Not surprisingly, students who are deep-elaborative processors "demonstrate faster learning, better memory, and higher grade point averages" (p. 385). Research in this area documents that:

. . .this type of learner attends more to the semantic features of material, whereas the repetitive and reiterative learners attend more to phonological and structural aspects. Shallow-reiterative information processors spend much of their study time repeating and memorizing information in its original form. They prefer to assimilate information as given rather than rewording, restating, or rethinking it (p. 385).

Thus, teachers should find ways to help students learn to adapt the style most appropriate to the material to be learned and to the type of testing, which would include helping them become deep-elaborative rather than shallow-reiterative processors.

If the classroom activities of the teacher tend to be deep and elaborative and if the homework exercises require the student to engage in deep and elaborative activities, then the immediate impact will be to counteract the less desirable effects of a shallow-reiterative learning style. The long-range effect may be a change in the student's learning style itself (p. 385).

Furthermore, tests are "major vehicles for shaping student learning styles. If we demand regurgitation, we encourage shallow, reiterative memorization; if we test for comprehension of meaning, we encourage deeper, more elaborative and thoughtful information processing" (p. 385).

Kolb

Another learning style differs from the others in that it was developed from a specific theory of learning called "experiential learning" (Kolb 1984). The theory deals not only with style but also with the more basic questions of learning and individual development. Drawing primarily on the works of Dewey (1938), who emphasized the need for learning to be grounded in experience, Lewin (1951), who stressed the importance of a person's being active in learning, and Piaget (1952), who described intelligence not so much as innate but rather the result of the interaction of the person and the environment, Kolb describes learning as a four-step process (see figure 4). Learners have immediate *concrete experience*, involving themselves fully in it and then reflecting on the experience from different perspectives. From these *reflective observations*, they en-

> **Thus, teachers should find ways to help students learn to adapt . . .which would include helping them become deep-elaborative rather than shallow-reiterative processors.**

gage in *abstract conceptualization*, creating generalizations or
principles that integrate their observations into sound theories.
Finally, learners use these generalizations or theories as guides
to further action, *active experimentation*, testing what they have
learned in new, more complex situations. The result is another
concrete experience, but this time at a more complex level.
Thus, the experiential learning theory is best thought of as a
helix, with learners having additional experiences, reflecting on
them, deducing generalizations about the experiences, and then
using them as guides to further action at increasing levels of
complexity.

Another way to look at the cycle is to distinguish between
what Kolb sees as the two fundamental elements in the learning
process. The first is grasping the experience or taking in information. Some people prefer grasping experience in concrete
ways, while others prefer doing so in ways that are more ab-

FIGURE 4

KOLB'S MODEL OF EXPERIENTIAL LEARNING

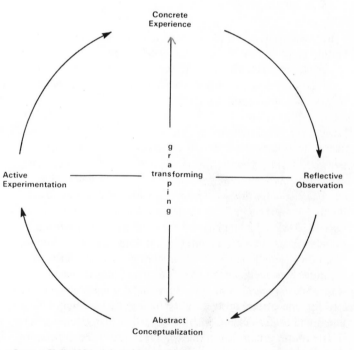

Source: Kolb 1984. Adapted by permission.

stract. The second element is processing or, more accurately, transforming the experience. Some tend to rely more on reflective observation, reflecting upon information essentially as it is. Others transform experience through active experimentation, changing the information or themselves to fit their thinking.

This grasping or prehending dimension of Kolb's model resonates with the basic "splitters" and "lumpers" categorized earlier. Kolb argues for a two-dimensional model of style, however, because he believes people have preferences as to how they transform their experience.

The four points on the experiential learning cycle, then, are modes of dealing with information or adapting to the world. To determine people's learning style, Kolb developed an inventory of learning styles (1976a, 1985) in which subjects rank order nine sets of four words (the 1976 version) or 12 stem completions (the 1985 version) concerning learning preferences (see figure 5).

The first group, "divergers," grasp the experience through concrete experience and transform it through reflective observation. Their major strength is their imaginative ability. They like to view situations from different perspectives and then weave many relationships into a meaningful whole. They are called divergers because they are good at generating ideas and brainstorming. They tend to be people oriented and emotional, and they often specialize in the humanities and the liberal arts.

The second group, "assimilators," grasp the experience through abstract conceptualization and transform it through reflective observation. Their primary strength is their ability to create theoretical models, and they are called assimilators because they like to assimilate diverse data into an integrated whole. They are less interested in people and are concerned about abstract concepts. They focus not so much on the practical application of ideas but on the soundness of the ideas or theories themselves.

Next are the "convergers," who grasp the experience through abstract conceptualization and transform it through active experimentation. Their strengths are the opposite of the divergers, and they are called convergers because, when presented with a question or task, they move quickly (converge) to find the one correct answer. They tend to be relatively unemotional and prefer dealing with things rather than people.

The fourth group, "accommodators," grasp the experience through concrete experience and transform it through active ex-

FIGURE 5
KOLB'S INVENTORY OF LEARNING STYLES

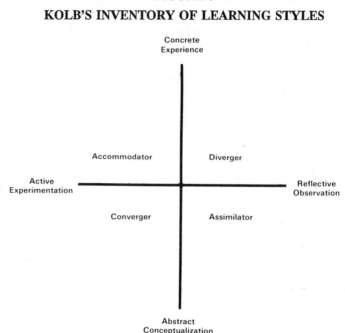

Concrete
Experience

Accommodator   Diverger

Active
Experimentation   Reflective
                                         Observation

Converger   Assimilator

Abstract
Conceptualization

Source: Kolb 1984. Adapted by permission.

perimentation. Their strengths are the opposite of the assimilators, and they like to focus on doing things and having new experiences. They are risk takers and are called accommodators because they do well in situations where they must adapt to meet new circumstances. They are intuitive, often using trial and error to solve problems. They are often impatient, even pushy, and when confronted with a theory that does not match the facts as they see them, they tend to discard the theory.

In a study of 800 managers and graduate students (1981b), Kolb found that the learning styles of the persons studied varied with their undergraduate major. Business majors tended to be accommodators, engineers tended to be convergers, history, English, psychology, and political science majors tended to be divergers, and mathematics, chemistry, economics, and sociology majors tended to be assimilators. Physics majors fell between convergers and assimilators.

✓ The critical link between learning and individual development is most clearly seen in the "cone," a visual representa-

tion in which Kolb integrates the four adaptive modes, the four
learning styles, and the movement from simplicity to greater
complexity in learning (see figure 6). The early years of one's
life (from infancy to about age 15) are a time of acquiring information and basic skills. A person is quite concrete, and the
self is experienced as undifferentiated and immersed in the
world. The next stage is one of specialization (about ages 16 to
40), in which the environment and one's own preferences
move the individual to greater specialization. People choose a
vocation, a place to live, and a field of study and begin to be
shaped by it. They begin to rely more on a particular style of
learning and become more skilled in the particular ways of

FIGURE 6
THE EXPERIENTIAL LEARNING THEORY OF
GROWTH AND DEVELOPMENT

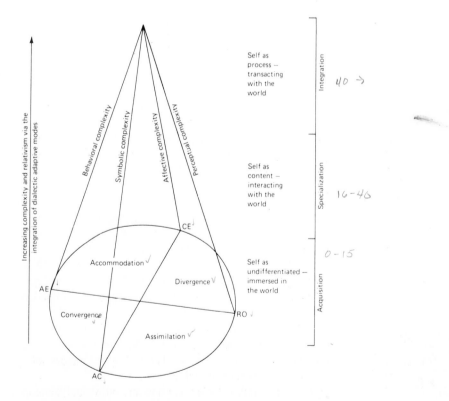

Source: Kolb 1984. Adapted by permission.

grasping and transforming experience. Here the self is defined as content as one interacts with the environment. In this stage, people move to specialization as a way of coping with a complex and multifaceted world. They develop competence in a particular area and thereby gain some degree of mastery and security. But that mastery comes at the price of personal fulfillment, because by specializing in one mode, a person may not develop increasing skill in others.

The third stage of development is called integration (about age 40 and beyond), a period that requires an existential confronting of the conflict between the need for specialized competence and the need for personal fulfillment. As part of the major shift that adults typically experience around mid-life, people feel a need to come to terms with their lives as they have experienced them thus far and to bring into play parts of themselves that have been relatively dormant (or suppressed) until then.

As to the adaptive modes, the direction of the shift depends on past and preferred modes. The person strong in reflective observation moves to active experimentation to become more of a shaper instead of being shaped. The person strong in active experimentation moves to reflective observation to reflect more instead of shaping. The person strong in abstract conceptualization moves to concrete experience to engage more instead of being detached. The person strong in concrete experience moves to abstract conceptualization to detach and analyze more instead of feeling and being enmeshed. The self begins to be experienced less as content and more as process and transacting with the world.

The cone is comprised of lines from the four adaptive modes extending upward to one point. From childhood to maturity, increasing complexity and relativism occur through the integration of the dialectical modes. Through the movement to greater complexity, relativism, and integration, learning enables one to reach the essence of the self. Kolb's thesis of human development, then, is that increasing competence and experience in all four adaptive modes lead to greater complexity, relativism, and integration. It argues clearly for the design of learning experiences that provide systematic opportunities for learners to deal with information in all four modes and to develop greater competence in each. If Kolb's thesis is correct, then the use of teaching practices that ensure the learner engages systematically in all four modes is not just a nice thing to do: It is a prerequisite for an effective society.

Research on Kolb's model of learning style and the experiential learning cycle compared a group of registered nurses working for a bachelor's degree with a group working for a nursing degree as well as a bachelor's degree (Lassan 1984). Findings indicated that the students were more similar in learning styles as they progressed toward the senior level. Both groups tended to become more competent in a diversity of learning modes rather than becoming fixed permanently in one learning style.

A longitudinal study to assess the cognitive development, learning styles, and generic abilities of college students found that during the course of their college careers, students move from a reliance upon concrete experience abilities to greater use of abstract conceptualization abilities (Mentkowski and Strait 1983). At the same time, the study showed, they changed somewhat from an emphasis on reflective observation to active experimentation.

It is to be expected that students would become more abstract as they move through their degree program; people typically move to greater abstraction as they grow older. Further, college curriculum is geared to this change and contains, by definition, an emphasis on abstraction. The move to greater active experimentation may be partly because the study was done at a college with a tradition of active learning that emphasizes applying theory to practice. And it may indicate that students become more active as learners, rather than relying on the somewhat less active stance of reflective observation.

Kolb's theory of learning style can be applied in portfolio development courses to stimulate self-discovery and interaction with others, to help students find their own learning strengths and weaknesses, and to stimulate conscious efforts in developing new potential for learning (Mark and Menson 1982). Researchers found that Kolb's model helped students enhance their learning experiences by providing a framework to discuss the learning process. The students in the study often reported an increased sense of self-esteem and self-understanding.

Information about learning style, such as that gained from Kolb's model, can be used to design management training programs (Dixon 1982). Knowing participants' learning style can aid in planning and evaluating workshops, making presentations and assignments, and applying knowledge to the work environment. Further, information about learning style can be useful to learners on the job as well as in the workshop itself, because learning on the job can be enhanced if workers understand more fully how they learn.

It is recommended that faculty members use the four models of the experiential learning cycle as a guide in the design of learning activities so that students systematically engage in each of them with the information to be learned (Murrell and Claxton 1987). In this way, the course is responsive to the four styles, because as the activities progress around the circle, all students "get the chance to 'shine' 25 percent of the time" (McCarthy 1981, p. 47). The assumption is that the most effective learning experience is one in which students have experiences in all four modes.

In the education of counselors, for example, a faculty member can have students engage in each of the four modes in helping them learn more about the roles and responsibilities of the professional counselor (Murrell and Claxton 1987). For concrete experience, students are required to interview a counselor who is currently practicing in an area where the student plans to work—an elementary or secondary school, a community agency, or a residential facility, for example. Once students have completed the interview and documented their findings, they engage in reflective observation to transform the information they have taken in. Structured group work in class provides the opportunity for questions: "How did you feel about doing the interview?" "How do you think the counselor feels about his or her job?" "How would you like to work in that setting?"

Next, students engage in abstract conceptualization and are asked to formulate questions they would like to have addressed in subsequent class sessions. For active experimentation, students are asked to write papers in which they recommend ways that agencies could serve their clients more effectively. In developing their papers, they draw on what they have learned in their interviews, in the class discussion, and from the information presented by the teacher.

Further, Kolb's cycle can be used to inform the design of examinations to assess students' abilities to think in ways that are divergent, assimilative, convergent and accommodative (Murrell and Claxton 1987). For example, open-ended test questions call on students to think in divergent ways as they generate alternative solutions to problems ("What are the various ways in which students in secondary schools could obtain information about careers?''). Questions that ask students to compare and contrast ideas or concepts test their skills in assimilative thinking (''Compare and contrast the counseling services found in the elementary school with those found in the secondary school.''). Questions that ask students to give specific information or to select the correct answer from alternatives provided call for convergent thinking (''Identify three theorists of the behavioral school.''). And questions the call for practical application of theoretical principles are accommodative in nature (''Describe the counseling services an agency could provide to children whose parents are in the process of getting a divorce and discuss how such services could be implemented.'').

Learning is enhanced as more of the modes are used (Stice 1987), increasing from 20 percent retention if only abstract conceptualization is used to 90 percent if all four modes are used (p. 293).

Does matching the teaching approach with the student's learning style lead to greater learning? Practically no research has been done with Kolb's inventory on that issue, but one study showed that achievement did not vary as a function of style (Ballard 1980) and another showed no association between learning styles and reactions to instructional methods (Fox 1984), calling into question the usefulness of the inventory and thus experiential learning theory as a guide to educational design.

Concerns about the validity and reliability of Kolb's inventory are important, and they have been the focus of considerable debate in the literature (Certo and Lamb 1980; Freedman and Stumpf 1978, 1980; Kolb 1981a; Stumpf and Freedman 1981). The instrument is more appropriate as a means of collecting aggregate data on students' styles than for individual prescription (Kolb 1976b, p. 13), and experience suggests that when the instrument is used for dialogic, rather than diagnostic, purposes, it is extremely useful.

Gregorc
A perspective similar to Kolb's model has been developed by Anthony Gregorc (1979), who believes that learning styles emerge from innate predispositions or proclivities and that people learn both through concrete experience and abstraction. In each of these modes, an individual may learn randomly or se-

Learning is enhanced as more of the modes are used, increasing from 20 percent retention if only abstract conceptualization is used to 90 percent if all four modes are used.

quentially. Gregorc considers each of these dualities as qualities that indicate how individuals relate to the world. Crossing the two main modes with each of the subdivisions produces a typology of patterns for learner preference: Concrete Sequential (CS), Concrete Random (CR), Abstract Sequential (AS), and Abstract Random (AR). While everyone exhibits all four patterns to some extent, most people have a predilection for one style or, at most, two.

Each style describes a different kind of learner (Gregorc and Ward 1977). Concrete sequential students have a propensity for deriving information through direct, hands-on experience. They appreciate order and logical sequence in presentation of material. Exhibiting a high level of sensory sensitivity, they prefer touchable, concrete materials in the classroom and specific, step-by-step directions, which they readily follow. Such students prefer workbooks, demonstration teaching, programmed instruction, and well-organized field trips.

Concrete random students approach learning with an experimental, trial-and-error attitude. They are more likely to have flashes of insight and make intuitive leaps in structured situations. They do not like step-by-step procedures that deny them opportunities to find their own way and work well independently or in small groups. These students prefer games, simulations, independent study projects, problem-solving activities, and optional assignments.

Abstract sequential students have strong skills in working with written and verbal symbols. They tend to think abstractly and use conceptual "pictures" as they learn. They are able to grasp concepts and ideas vicariously. They prefer to learn through reading and listening and profit from orderly, rational presentations given by authorities.

Abstract random students are tuned to nuances of mood and atmosphere. They tend to associate the medium with the message and link a speaker's manner of delivery and personality to the content of what is being related. Thus, they globally evaluate the learning experience. Abstract random students prefer to receive information in an unstructured manner and like group discussions and multisensory experiences free from rules and guidelines. Thus, they prefer movies, group discussion, question-and-answer sessions, and television.

Some research has studied institutional effects on dental students' learning style—whether styles are affected by a school's educational philosophy, teaching methods, testing procedures, and curricular arrangements (Hendricson, Berlocher, and Herbert 1987). Gregorc's Learning Style Delineator was administered four times in a longitudinal, four-year study to 48 students.

Results of the study showed that most of the students were concrete sequential, a finding that was consistent with an earlier cross-sectional study. Such students typically prefer concrete sequential learning environments that are highly structured with well-defined learning tasks. They prefer logically sequenced topics and a curriculum with a practical orientation. Thus, it appears that the learning environment did not substantially alter students' learning styles but that learning styles remain relatively stable over time. Further, students' learning styles are primarily a by-product of the institution's selection process rather than caused by the institution.

These findings have three important implications. First, the general learning environment at this institution was consistent with students' learning preferences. Second, while concrete sequential was the dominant learning style, 20 to 30 percent of the students preferred abstract sequential, thus posing a challenge to the dental faculty to develop ways to provide a better learning environment for those students. Third, the marked preference of present students for concrete sequential learning may be at odds with the shift in emphasis in dental education from restoration dentistry to the diagnosis and prevention of periodontal disease. The latter is far more conceptual and may place increased burdens on the present type of students who are comfortable with more concrete learning.

***

Several important findings emerge from this discussion of information-processing models of learning style. All are at least reminiscent of lumpers and splitters, reinforcing Kirby's view that much of the research on style may be dealing with just two fundamental aspects of the personality and parallels split-brain research (Kolb 1984, pp. 46–51).

Schmeck's model brings up a very important issue that has not yet been discussed: the interaction of style and developmental stage. At times the two seem to be the same thing. For example, shallow-reiterative thinking sounds very much like the thinking of students who are at an earlier stage of development, while deep-elaborative processing sounds like the thinking of persons who are at a higher, more complex stage of development. The two concepts are not the same, but their interaction is so close that it is difficult to keep them separate.

Schmeck is certainly correct in recommending that faculty provide learning activities and tests that encourage shallow-reiterative students to learn to engage in deep-elaborative ways. But when Schmeck's model is used to describe persons at different stages, asking students to engage in deep-elaborative thinking with its emphasis on generating personal examples that relate to the issue and seeing the issue from different perspectives is a task students at early developmental stages simply may not be able to do. Nevertheless, if students are at a stage of cognitive development such that they are unable to move beyond their "surface-atomistic" approach, then that is how they see the world (Perry 1986, p. 190). Their view at least deserves faculty members' respect, for, to state the obvious, they can change only as fast as they can change. "Our success [as faculty members interested in student development] will be in proportion to our respect for the students' 'resistance' (that is, felt integrity)" (p. 193).

Thus, faculty need to be as insightful as possible concerning students' style and developmental stage. If students can focus only on memorization and processing information in somewhat shallow ways, they need to be allowed to do so. At the same time, however, faculty need to provide activities and assignments that stimulate students' movement to deeper thinking, so long as it is done in a way that respects their integrity.

The research on dental students' learning styles (Hendricson, Berlocher, and Herbert 1987) points out that all institutions need to be aware of their students' primary learning orientation and how it interacts with curricular emphases and emerging curricular trends. Just as the changing mix of students may call for teaching that is more field sensitive, so too may changing curricular emphases force faculty to be more aware of learning styles generally.

The most effective learners are those who have skills both in description building and in procedure building, and all students should have at least some skill in learning when the sequence is reversed. Thus, one of the most significant uses of learning style is for faculty to be aware of students' strengths and to help them gain insight into their competence so they can use it to full advantage. At the same time, faculty should find ways to help students learn in ways that are not their preferred style.

By providing activities that are a mismatch, students are able to become more skilled learners.

A cautionary note needs to be added, however. Having students learn in ways that are not consistent with their "natural" approach can be very threatening. In those instances, faculty need to be guided by the view that teaching is, more than anything else, "a caring stance in the moving context of our students' lives" (Daloz 1986, p. 14).

This issue of helping students develop new ways of learning comes into clearer focus with the work of Kolb. Because learning styles and the experiential learning cycle are anchored in human development research, his model enables us to be quite systematic and intentional about designing courses that not only foster development but also enable students to be actively involved in the learning process, a key recommendation of the report of the National Institute of Education on the need for improvement in higher education (1984). Mentkowski and Strait's longitudinal study indicates that curricular experiences help students move to greater abstraction, an extremely important ability for effective functioning as an adult. It also demonstrates that students' learning experiences can help them expand their repertoire of learning strategies. This empowering experience—"learning how to learn" (Smith 1982)—is a critical ingredient in a student's college experience, and it—in addition to solid mastery of content—is the assumption behind the recommendation that courses be designed to engage students in the four modes of the experiential learning cycle (Murrell and Claxton 1987).

The finding that use of Kolb's model in portfolio development courses helped students develop a greater appreciation of their strengths and become more intentional about learning in the future is an important one. It, too, suggests the use of information about learning styles as a means of empowering students. This perspective can be extremely significant for colleges that are serious about helping students take increasing charge of their own learning and of their own lives.

Social-Interaction Models
Mann's research
The first model discussed in this section grew out of a pioneering study at the University of Michigan that involved four undergraduate classes in psychology (Mann et al. 1970). The classes, made up of 47 women and 49 men, were all lecture-

discussion sections of an introductory psychology class taught by four instructors who each had had just one semester of prior university teaching experience. The data were gathered through extensive interviews of students and teachers and use of the 16-category, member-leader scoring system (Mann, Gibbard, and Hartman 1967). This system includes impulse areas (hostility and affection), authority relations areas (dominance and dependence), and ego state areas (anxiety, self-esteem, and depression). Trained observers scored each session of the classes.

Through factor analysis, the researchers identified eight clusters of students based on their behavior in the classroom: compliant students, anxious-dependent students, discouraged workers, independent students, heroes, snipers, attention seekers, and silent students. While classes vary, students change, and no person fits perfectly into one typology, these clusters can nevertheless help teachers see their students as fully complex individuals rather than as an undifferentiated group.

Cluster one, the compliant students, were mostly freshmen. They were the typical "good students" who adapted themselves to the will of authorities and conformed to standards. Seeing the teacher as the dispenser of extrinsic rewards, their main concern was understanding the material. They were very task oriented, nonrebellious, and accepting of what the teacher said. Although they performed reasonably well in class, they were not particularly innovative, creative, or intellectual.

Cluster two, the anxious-dependent students, was a larger group than the compliant students. They were angry on the inside and frightened on the outside, dependent on the teacher for knowledge and support, and anxious about being evaluated. Their past lives had not been particularly happy, having experienced a mix of parental affection and high standards as children. They were easily hurt and tried to win love through accepting and following the standards set by persons in authority. Their scores on standardized tests of verbal ability were lower than other clusters, which may account for their low regard for their intellectual competence. They were easily silenced by punitiveness on the part of the teacher and unable to become involved in the material or to look at it from an independent point of view.

Cluster three, the discouraged workers, was also a small cluster. These students had a mix of self-esteem and strength as well as guilt and depression. They were dissatisfied with themselves, had a pervasive feeling of guilt, and were generally depressed about human nature and the future in general. They were preoccupied with their inner selves, lacked sensitivity to others, and had fantasies that they might hurt others.

Cluster four, the independent students, was made up of older students, mostly sophomores and juniors. They were very intelligent, secure, and comfortable, able to see the class's activities and material with a certain detachment. They were not interested in intense personal relationships with the teacher. They were capable of thinking critically and had an individualistic perspective. In their relations with other class members, they were rather aloof.

Cluster five was the heroes. Their work in the class was tied to rebellion. They felt superior and saw themselves as exceptional persons whose lives were apart from and beyond the common people. They had the highest college board scores of all the eight groups, yet they were underachievers with grade averages of just over "C." They tended not to be anxious or dependent and had the ability and the willingness to help the teacher when he was uncomfortable. They saw the university as an oppressive system and distrusted authorities. They had the ability to defeat the teacher in an argument and at times insisted on doing so. They desired closeness with others yet were threatened by it at the same time.

Cluster six, the snipers, was much like the heroes, but their rebelliousness was more expressive and defensive. Under-achievers with low self-esteem, they were likely to address hostile comments to the teacher. Their investment in the class was low and, combined with the need to rebel, led to a kind of sniping at the teacher. They were pessimistic about relations with authority figures and the future and needed to remain uninvolved with the class and with major substantive issues. They were unhappy as children; their fathers were authoritarian yet weak.

Cluster seven, the attention seekers, had a predominantly social orientation and were frequently involved in joking, talking, showing off, and bragging. They tended to enjoy—and needed to be with—other people. Their interest in social interaction rather than in work inhibited their intellectual development. They were preoccupied with the appearance of things, how others perceived them, and the impression they made on the teacher, and they relied heavily on others' standards in forming their own judgments.

Cluster eight, the silent students, was a very large group,

characterized not so much by what they did but by what they did not do. They had a tremendous sense of helplessness and vulnerability, were suspicious, almost paranoid, and could be very disconcerting to others. The males were angry and defensive, believing the teacher was a threat to their identity yet yearning for the teacher's affection and attention. The females acted out the stereotypical feminine sex role—"good little girls are seen but not heard." Their parents were emotionally distant or physically absent, giving them so little feedback they had no accurate evaluation of their behavior. Because their self-worth was deeply tied up with the work they did in class, they spent an inordinate amount of time trying to figure out what the teacher wanted. These students wanted attention and to be center stage very badly, but their fear of failure was so great they preferred to remain silent.

Grasha and Reichmann

Another mode, based on students' response styles, was developed over a period of two years in interviews with students at the University of Cincinnati (Grasha 1972; Reichmann and Grasha 1974). Three styles emerged during the interviews: avoidant participant, competitive-collaborative, and dependent-independent. The response styles were defined around three classroom dimensions: student's attitudes toward learning, their views of the teacher and/or peers, and their reaction to classroom procedures.

Subsequently, Grasha and Reichmann developed the Grasha-Reichmann Student Learning Style Scales (GRSLSS) by using a "rational" approach to scale construction.[2] The instrument was developed with the assistance of undergraduate students who were asked to sort student behaviors in a typical classroom into the six student response styles. The learning styles thus developed are as follows:

1. *Independent students* like to think for themselves. They prefer working on their own but will listen to others. They are confident of their ability to learn and will learn what they feel is needed.
2. *Dependent students* have little intellectual curiosity and learn only what is required. They see the teacher as a

[2]For a discussion of the "rational" approach to scale construction, see Jackson 1971.

source of structure and support and look to authorities to be told what to do.

3. *Collaborative students* like learning through sharing with others. They are cooperative and enjoy working with others, and they see the classroom as a place for learning and for interaction with others.

4. *Competitive students* feel they must compete with others for reward, and their motivation to learn is to do better than others. They regard the classroom as strictly a win-lose situation in which they must win.

5. *Participant students* desire to learn course content and enjoy attending class. They assume responsibility for getting a lot out of class and participate with others when told to do so. They do little that is not required, however.

6. *Avoidant students* do not participate in the class actively and are not interested in learning course content.

Grasha and Reichmann have developed classroom activity preferences for each style. Competitive students, for example, are comfortable with a variety of teaching methods, so long as the focus is teacher centered rather than student centered. They enjoy serving as group leaders in discussions or when working on projects. Collaborative students prefer lectures, with class discussion in small groups and talking with others outside class about issues dealt with in the course. Avoidant students are generally negative about any classroom activities. They would prefer self-evaluation for grading and do not like enthusiastic teachers. Participant students prefer lectures with discussion, enjoy teachers who can analyze and synthesize material well, and like opportunities to discuss material. Dependent students want the teacher to outline for assignments, and to use teacher-centered classroom methods. Independent students enjoy self-paced instruction, assignments that give them a chance to think for themselves, and a student-centered rather than a teacher-centered classroom setting.

The GRSLSS was used in a study of the interrelationship of teaching methods, preferred learning styles, and learning outcomes (Andrews 1981). Freshmen students in an introductory chemistry course at the University of California at San Diego were randomly assigned to two types of sections taught by teaching assistants. In the instructor-centered sections, the instructor provided minilectures, answered questions for students, worked problems, and questioned students; that is, the instructor played a central role in guiding the class. In the peer-centered section, the instructor served more as a facilitator and a resource, emphasizing students' responsibility for presentations and student-to-student teaching.

In administering the GRSLSS to students, the researcher predicted that students who scored high on the collaborative dimension of the scales would find the peer-centered format more beneficial and that those who scored high on the competitive dimension would benefit more from the instructor-centered format. At the end of the course, students completed a questionnaire asking for their reaction to the section meeting and their rating of the learning benefit they received. Course grades on the mid-term and final were used as a means of judging overall learning performance.

Analysis of the data revealed that "the two sections were approximately equal in learning, except that more learning from fellow students occurred in the peer-centered sections" (Andrews 1981, p. 161). As expected, the peer-centered method was "clearly the most beneficial for collaboratively oriented students, while the competitive individuals felt they learned better in the instructor-centered sections" (p. 170). Thus, "students learn best in settings that meet their social-emotional needs and are attuned to their predominant pattern of behavior" (p. 178).

Fuhrmann and Jacobs
Another model and instrument, the Fuhrmann-Jacobs model, involves three styles: dependent, collaborative, and independent (Fuhrmann and Grasha 1983, pp. 114–21). According to the model, no one style is bad because each is appropriate for different contexts or situations. In a situation where students have little or no prior knowledge or experience, a dependent style is to be expected and is therefore appropriate. In a course that emphasizes group problem solving, a collaborative approach probably makes the most sense. Personality is an important force in using style as well. Some students are more independent and will likely choose a more independent means of accomplishing a learning objective if given the option of doing so. Table 1 lists descriptions of learners' needs, the teacher's role, and appropriate teaching behavior for each style.

Eison
The last model discussed in this section, developed by Eison (1979), identifies style in terms of students' attitudes toward

grading and learning. Although the framework was derived from attitudes toward grades rather than from observation of behavior in the classroom, those attitudes are often manifest in behavior. Hence, it is included in this section on social-interaction models. Eison's early work was based on the idea that students seemed to fall into two categories: (1) learning-oriented (LO) students, who see the classroom as a place where they anticipate finding information and ideas that will be important to them; and (2) grade-oriented (GO) students, who see the classroom as a place where they will be tested and graded and that they must endure to obtain a degree or certification. Eison developed an instrument called LOGO (Learning Orientation, Grade Orientation) to assess students' positions on this scale.

Personality is an important force in using style as well.

Using the instrument in conjunction with other indicators of psychological type, general personality traits, study habits and attitudes, and locus of control, he found that students who were high in learning orientation and low in grade orientation had more positive attitudes toward education and better study habits. They appeared to be more self-motivated and inner directed, experienced less debilitating test anxiety, and were more interested in new ideas and intellectual matters than other students. In contrast, students who scored high in grade orientation and low in learning orientation tended to act in conventional ways and had a realistic and tough-minded approach to personal concerns. These students experienced a great deal of test anxiety and were least likely to have effective study practices.

A second instrument developed several years later, LOGO II, refines the original one and results in a fourfold typology of orientations:

1. *High Learning Orientation/High Grade Orientation* (High LO/High GO). Such students are typically in the premed or prelaw curriculum, and they are highly motivated both to learn and to achieve high grades.
2. *High Learning Orientation/Low Grade Orientation* (High LO/Low GO). These students are in school for educational enrichment and personal growth.
3. *Low Learning Orientation/High Grade Orientation* (Low LO/High GO). These students' primary interest in class is to get a good grade.
4. *Low Learning Orientation/Low Grade Orientation* (Low

TABLE 1
STUDENT AND TEACHER DESCRIPTORS

Learner's Style	Learner's Needs	Teacher's Role	Teacher's Behavior
Dependent (may occur in introductory courses, languages, some sciences, when learner has little or no information upon entering course)	Structure Direction External reinforcement Encouragement Esteem from authority	Expert Authority	Lecturing Demonstrating Assigning Checking Encouraging Testing Reinforcing Transmitting content Designing materials Grading
Collaborative (may occur when learner has some knowledge, information, and ideas and would like to share them or try them out)	Interaction Practice Probe self and others Observation Peer challenge Peer esteem Experimentation	Co-learner Environment setter Participation	Interacting Questioning Providing resources Modeling Providing feedback Coordinating Evaluating Managing Observing processes Grading
Independent (may occur when learner has much more knowledge or skill upon entering the course and wants to continue to search on own; may feel instructor cannot offer as much as he or she would like)	Internal awareness Experimentation Time Nonjudgmental support	Facilitator	Allowing Providing requested feedback Providing resources Consulting Listening Negotiating Evaluating

©1980 Ronne Jacobs and Barbara Fuhrmann. Reprinted by permission.

LO/Low GO). Such students are often in college only to have a good time or to avoid getting a job (Milton, Pollio, and Eison 1986).

A question frequently asked is whether the learning styles of traditional-age students are different from those of adult students. Four scales were used—LOGO, the GRSLSS, the survey of study habits and attitudes (Brown and Holtzman 1967), and the achievement anxiety test (Alpert and Haber 1960)—in a study of 272 students in 10 sections of an introductory psychology course at a two-year college (Eison and Moore 1980). For purposes of analysis, students were divided into three groups: traditional age (17–22), young adults (23–31), and older adults (32–67). The researchers found, first, that the young adults and older adults scored significantly higher on the LOGO scale than those in the traditional age group, which means that "adult students are more likely to be oriented toward the pursuit of knowledge than...concerned with merely working for a course grade" (pp. 6–7). In terms of test anxiety, younger students were more likely to experience greater tension and anxiety than students in the other age groups.

The results suggest that younger students may well "prefer such activities as (a) short, frequent quizzes drawn from clearly specified study questions, (b) graded assignments (rather than nongraded learning activities), and (c) extra-credit activities to help raise one's score. Adults, on the other hand, might (a) be less concerned with the instructor's testing policy, (b) enjoy less structured, ungraded, learning opportunities, and (c) worry less about what their final course grade might be" (p. 10).

The learning styles of traditional-age students were significantly different from the other age groups as measured by the Grasha-Reichmann Student Learning Style Scales. Along the dimension of avoidant, competitive, and participant, the styles of the younger students "were characterized by (a) generally lower levels of interest in the course, (b) higher levels of competitive feelings toward other students, and (c) decreased interest in assuming responsibility for getting the most out of class or participating with others" (p. 8). Thus, concluded the authors, interesting younger students in "traditional course material and involving them in learning activities may prove a more difficult challenge for the instructor than working with adult students" (p. 10).

Because younger students are more competitive in their

orientation toward the classroom, activities that are rewarded through grades or other means may have great appeal to them. On the other hand, older students seem to be high on the participant scale and apparently want to participate as much as possible in class-related activities. "They enjoy lively, enthusiastic presentation of material, especially when the instructor can analyze and synthesize material well, followed by class discussions" (p. 10).

***

Two kinds of motivation in students may relate to the orientations to learning Eison describes (Chickering and Havighurst 1981). The first is instrumental, where a person engages in an activity to achieve a practical payoff. For example, a person studies the rules of safe driving to pass the examination to get a driving license. The second motivation is developmental or expressive, where the reward is in the act itself. For example, one visits an art museum not for pragmatic reasons but for the pleasure and the learning that are involved in the visit.

Grade-oriented students seem to be extremely instrumental in their view of their courses. While this attitude can be very frustrating to faculty, they should not be surprised. Human development theory says that many students, especially those in the traditional age range, are very instrumental. One should bear in mind, however, that "instrumental" and "developmental" are not dichotomous. Rather, instrumental achievement can contribute to development, and growth in developmental areas enables students to expand their instrumental competence as well. Hence, the grade orientation of students is not to be denigrated, for achievement in that area, when handled in a sensitive and insightful way, can lead students to an increased sense of competence. And as a sense of competence builds, the chances increase that students can move to a more developmental orientation with respect to themselves and their education.

Instructional-Preference Models
The research of Hill
This section presents learning style models that are concerned with students' preferences for particular teaching methods. A widely known and used model is cognitive style mapping, developed by the late Joseph E. Hill and his associates at Oakland Community College in Bloomfield Hills, Michigan (Hill and Nunnery 1973). Hill, who was president at Oakland, be-

lieved it was possible to develop an underlying structure and scientific language for education. He developed a comprehensive framework he called the "educational sciences," which include (1) *symbols and their meanings*, which are based on the belief that people use theoretical and qualitative symbols basic to the acquisition of knowledge and meaning; (2) *cultural determinants* of the meanings of symbols, which are concerned with the cultural influences that affect what the symbols mean to particular individuals; (3) *modalities of influence*, which are the elements that show how a person makes inferences; (4) biochemical and electrophysiological aspects of *memory-concern*, (5) *cognitive style*, which is the product of the first four sciences, (6) *teaching, counseling, and administrative style*, and (7) *systematic analysis decision making*.

Hill's model, or shorter forms of it, is being used with students from elementary school through graduate school in institutions throughout the country. With instruments that include the elements listed in the previous paragraph, a student's learning style can be "mapped" and interpreted.

Assessments of cognitive style have been offered at the University of Texas Health Science Center in Dallas "as an aid to first-year medical students experiencing difficulty to help them more efficiently deal with the massive information presented, and also as an aid to the staff, providing them a positive way to counsel the student" (Ehrhardt 1983, p. 571). Mapping has been found to be useful in preparing continuing education courses for physicians at the University of Texas Medical Branch at Galveston. It can also be useful in clinical laboratory sciences and other settings. "Churches, discussion groups, management teams, professionals, youth organizations, and graduate classes have all made good use of cognitive style as a topic" (p. 571).

Does providing students with learning experiences that match their style as measured by Hill's instrument lead to improved learning? In one study, 51 community college students enrolled in an audiotutorial course were given pre- and post-tests to determine their level of anxiety (Terrell 1976). Their cognitive style of learning was also determined. It was found that students whose cognitive styles matched the instructional mode tended to achieve higher grades and experienced greater reduction in anxiety than the nonmatched students.

Hill's model has also been used as part of a study to help students become more independent in their learning (Flippo and

Terrell 1984). Previous research had indicated that prescriptive programs in reading tended to foster in students a dependency upon others for guidance in their studies. In this study, the researchers studied students working on reading and study skills in the Developmental Center at the University of South Carolina. They asked whether the students in a program intentionally geared to their particular needs would use information on their cognitive style to take greater charge of their own skill development. In the "prescriptive" group, students were given clear direction on what they were to do. The researchers administered Hill's cognitive style mapping instrument to the students in the "personalized" group and helped them understand the results. They provided examples of how to use that understanding in working on developmental materials and in other classes. The staff of the center was available to assist in understanding their style but did not prescribe activities for them.

The results of the study showed that the students in the "personalized" group had a more positive attitude toward skill development and more self-confidence about their potential in college. They indicated that their knowledge of styles was useful to them in gaining greater skill in reading and studying and in other college work generally. The authors noted that it took only an hour to administer the cognitive style mapping procedure, a modest investment considering the important results it had for the students.

With the rapidly expanding and exciting potential of education through the use of technology, an important area for research is the role of learning style where the student and teacher communicate not in person but via teleview, telephone, or computer. One researcher asked whether cognitive style mapping would be helpful in predicting which students would complete a telecourse in English in a community college and whether students with particular styles would do better academically (Rice 1984). While the data were not useful in predicting success or failure in the telecourse, patterns in the data could be used "to predict whether a student perseveres or withdraws 83 percent of the time" (p. 3517-A).

Another study was conducted to determine whether students who were mapped and had their learning style explained to them would make better grades (Fourier 1980). The Albany instrument (a modification of the educational cognitive style inventory researched by the Center for Curriculum and Instruction, State University of New York at Albany) was administered to students in 31 sections of natural science, social science, and humanities at a community college. The results of their maps were discussed with the students, along with suggestions about strategies they could employ in their courses. A control group received a placebo treatment, and the teachers in the various class sections were not aware of the experiment. The results showed that students in the experimental group achieved significantly higher grades in the course than the control group.

An evaluation of the mapping program at Mountain View Community College indicates that students felt their maps had given them helpful information on how they learned, many had actually changed the way they studied, and they expected to select course sections on the basis of the mapping experience. Faculty members said mapping was worth the time involved, assisted them in understanding students' learning styles, and helped them see how to make needed changes in their instruction (Sims and Ehrhardt 1978).

A recurrent problem in higher education is getting innovative practices institutionalized so that they become integral to the workings of the college and the teachers. The experiences of three community colleges that have worked with cognitive style mapping for several years are instructive in this regard.

The goal of President Hill at Oakland Community College was, first, to help students understand their own style and, second, to have five learning modes available from which students could choose when enrolling in their courses: lecture, individualized program learning, videotapes, audiotapes, and small group seminars with peer tutoring (Kirby 1979, pp. 59–65). Thus, the institution had to make some very substantial changes to accommodate students' diverse styles. The goal of having five modes or paths was never realized. Dr. Hill died in 1978, and one wonders "whether the movement will continue with the vigor it once enjoyed despite the removal of the one person upon whom so much of it rested" (p. 65).

William O'Mahoney, dean of academic affairs at Oakland, indicates that it did not. "Over the years other problems and concerns have moved to the fore. Further, faculty have found that it takes a huge amount of time and energy to truly individualize the learning process for students. To do that on a massive scale is very difficult."*

Reports from Mountain View Community College and Mt.

*William O'Mahoney 1987, personal communication.

Hood Community College are more encouraging. Jim Corby, dean of the learning resource center at Mountain View, states that the use of learning styles is now fully institutionalized.† In the early days, certain resources were specifically allocated to a large program of mapping students and teachers. Students were helped to understand their own style, select course sections consistent with the style, and develop strategies for succeeding in courses where a mismatch occurred. Corby believes so much activity occurred several years ago that it became part of most faculty members' thinking. "The system runs pretty much on its own now, without a lot of care and feeding." When professors want to map their students, they get the materials from the campus testing center, administer them to students in class, and then have them scored. The professors explain the results to the class, and together they discuss instructional plans for the semester. They can then change the plans, based on the results of the mapping and the ensuing discussion with the class.

Jack Miller, dean of instruction at Mt. Hood, reports that several years ago a lot of high-visibility activities occurred around cognitive style mapping.†† At one time, for example, the college published the schedule for each term and included a two-line annotation on each course section provided by the professors (who had themselves been mapped) on how the course would be taught. Students who knew their style could then select the course section in which they wished to enroll. This procedure exemplifies the college's strong commitment to helping students succeed, a particularly important trait for an open-admissions institution.

The primary vehicle for institutionalization of learning styles at Mt. Hood today is a one-hour course in psychology titled "College and Career Planning." It is required of all full-time enrollees, and part-time students are encouraged to take it as well. In the course, students are to be mapped and to learn about their own style, to develop a program of courses for the two full years and become familiar with all college services, such as counseling, advising, and placement, and to receive assistance in such areas as study skills and time management.

"The existence of the course is an example of Mt. Hood's broad commitment to effective teaching," states Dean Miller.

†Jim Corby 1987, personal communication.
††Jack Miller 1987, personal communication.

Its development came from the efforts of the division of academic affairs working with the division of student affairs, a contrast to the practice in many institutions, where little joint effort is devoted to promoting students' learning. "In a way," says Miller, "learning style has become a common ground for the two divisions."

The college has an institutionwide student success task force that gives guidance to the faculty who teach the course. A professional development workshop is held each fall for the faculty who teach the course. Faculty are thus able to stay abreast of current information about problems students typically have, new services being offered, and improved strategies for teaching.

Canfield

The second model in the instructional-preference category is, like Hill's model, quite comprehensive. An industrial psychologist drew on his extensive practical experiences in assisting colleges with improving students' learning and on research to develop the Canfield Learning Style Inventory (Canfield 1980). Two key theoretical areas that informed his work were Maslow's hierarchy of needs and McClelland's research on achievement motivation.

Canfield developed scales in four areas. The first area is concerned with the *conditions of learning*, including *affiliation* (or the student's need to develop personal relationships with other students and the instructor), *structure* (their desire for organization and detail), *achievement* (their desire for setting goals and for independence), and *eminence* (their orientation toward competition and authority).

The second area deals with students' preferences in terms of *content*, including *numerics* (working with numbers and logic), *qualitative* (working with words or language), *inanimate* (working with things, such as in building or repairing), and *people* (working with people, such as in interviewing and sales).

The third area assesses students' preferences in terms of *mode: listening, reading, iconic,* and *direct experience*.

The last area is students' *expectations* as to the grades they thought they would receive. This variable has been found to be extremely important in terms of what students will achieve.

The Canfield Instructional Style Inventory considers generally the same dimensions as the learning style instrument (Canfield and Canfield 1986). The clear interface between the two

Students were helped to understand their own style, select course sections consistent with the style, and develop strategies for succeeding in courses where a mismatch occurred.

provides a context in which students and faculty can talk about course design and learning activities.

A study of students at Miami-Dade Community College found that students who were taught in ways that matched their learning style achieved higher reading scores and perceived their educational experience more positively (Canfield 1980). A study of learning styles and teaching styles of mathematics students and instructors found that students with higher grades in the course had learning styles that more clearly related to the teachers' instructional styles than did the students who received lower grades (Canfield 1980). And another study, of the learning styles of developmental students in English, reading, and mathematics, found that students who were low in the desire for peer affiliation tended to be the most successful, that performance in English was positively related to preference for reading, and that students who preferred numerics tended to do better in mathematics (Canfield 1980).

In a study comparing the learning style preferences of 1,064 older students (28 years or older) with 1,760 younger students (23 years or younger), younger students were found to be more affiliative (Ommen, Brainard, and Canfield 1979). Further, older students preferred traditional instructional formats (listening, reading, organized and detailed materials, and less independence), while younger students preferred iconics and direct experience as learning modes and had lower expectation of doing well.

The Canfield instrument was used in teaching classes in engineering at Triton College, a two-year institution in Illinois (Brillhart 1981). The instructor developed a student profile that related ACT scores, results of the Strong-Campbell Interest Inventory, and data about learning style. The results of the Canfield instrument administered to 312 students showed that, in terms of the four modes of learning, most students preferred the listening and direct experiences modes, accepted iconic, and resisted reading. The instructor was able to structure the course to be responsive to students' learning style.

Learning style played an important role in another study at Triton concerning an interdisciplinary course developed by the same instructor and a rhetoric teacher (Brillhart and Debs 1982). They collected data with the Canfield Learning Style Inventory and other instruments to develop a profile of students in an engineering-rhetoric course. The two teachers also completed the inventories themselves to assess their own learning styles, as they assumed that how they learned and how they taught showed direct correlation. The results indicated their styles "bracketed" the students' own styles; that is, between the two of them, their styles reflected the diverse learning preferences of their students.

Because the student profile revealed a wide range of competencies and learning styles, the course included several different teaching methodologies and assignments. It included "at least 25 writing assignments and 36 related activities, varying in condition, mode, content, and performance expectations. The combined presence of two faculty members from diverse backgrounds accentuated the mixture of teaching and learning styles" (p. 83).

A group project met the needs many of the students had for peer affiliation. To meet the preference many had for authority eminence, videotapes of nationally recognized engineers were used. Because many of the students were trying to decide about career options, opportunities were presented for personal interviews with practicing engineers, an activity linked to the preference of many students for direct experience. The course had a clear structure and sequence, and students were thus aware of the teachers' expectations.

Final evaluations of the course, which was taught for four years, showed that: (1) students achieved higher levels of competence; (2) they rated the course among the highest of courses ever taken; and (3) engineering students with both very low and very high ACT scores did much better in the second-semester rhetoric course than the engineering students with similar ACT scores who had taken the standard entry-level rhetoric course.

***

The research on instructional-preference models lends weight to the idea that matching instructional methods to students' learning style can lead to improved learning, but the studies in this section reveal other important findings as well. First, gathering data on students' learning style can strengthen a teacher's ability to identify students who will not do well. While the finding that students who prefer reading will do well in English and those who prefer numerics will do well in math is not surprising, it suggests that those who have very low preference in these areas are more likely to do poorly and thus deserve special attention and effort from the teacher.

The finding that information from cognitive style mapping provides a way to predict persistence is similarly important. Such information, coupled with a profile of data on learning style and on other information as well, helps teachers to teach with a surer hand. Such studies also point up the fact that data about learning style need to be considered in the context of other information. A comprehensive approach is necessary, for "data from a single source lead to dichotomous thinking" (Mentkowski 1987).

This line of reasoning relates well to the need for "classroom research" (Cross 1987). It is incorrect to assume that traditional educational research, with its emphasis on data gathered across classes and institutions that are then analyzed and reported in professional journals, will have much effect on the behavior of most college faculty. If teachers see themselves more as persons whose research efforts include the teaching-learning process itself, however, they could generate modest amounts of data to produce excellent results, for the information would be directly applicable to *this* group of students at *this* particular time. Information about learning style has the added advantage of being relatively nontechnical and esoteric, and it is thus of greater practical value to teachers whose major expertise is in their discipline, not in research methodology.

Second, the issue of learning how to learn is underscored by the indication that students who learn about their own style achieve higher grades and have more positive attitudes about their studies, greater self-confidence, and more skill in applying their knowledge in college courses generally. Much of the effort on cajoling faculty to teach in different ways (efforts that often result in little change) might be better directed toward helping students become more sophisticated and skilled in how to learn in different contexts. And because teachers themselves find it helpful to know more about how their students learn and how to make needed changes in instruction, it may be that the long-term impact of learning style is the increase in achievement and self-confidence that comes about when faculty and students engage in an ongoing dialogue about how the student learns, how the teacher teaches, and how each can adapt to the other in the service of more effective learning.

Third, the many years of experience at Oakland, Mountain View, and Mt. Hood help us see how to promote the institutionalization of the use of learning style. When resources and procedures are in place to help faculty use information about learning style and do so with only a modest amount of effort, the concept continues to be important. And when the academic division and the student services division work together and the institution establishes a required, credit-bearing course that is updated through regular review and continuing faculty development, learning style is accepted as an important part of an array of efforts designed to promote students' success.

What does the literature say about the use of research on learning style in key areas of students' development? The Schmeck model of deep-elaborative processing/shallow-reiterative processing was used in a study of 30 undergraduates who volunteered to talk with counselors for two sessions about personal problems (McCarthy, Shaw, and Schmeck 1986). Drawing on the language of Piaget, the researchers noted that the task of counselors is to encourage clients "to process current experiences by bringing old schemata to bear (assimilation) and, when necessary, encourage the revision of the schemata (accommodation),...precisely the types of activity that Schmeck (1983) referred to as deep and elaborative processing" (p. 250).

The purpose of the study was to determine whether counselors and two other professionals would correctly classify those counseled as deep-elaborative or shallow-reiterative processors, solely on the basis of the clients' verbal behavior. The researchers hypothesized that the verbal protocols of the deep-elaborative subjects would be judged as deeper, more elaborative, clearer, more personal, and more conclusion oriented and that the protocols of the shallow-reiterative processors would be judged as more shallow, nonelaborative, description oriented, impersonal, and vague.

The results of the study indicated that the counselor and other professionals were indeed able to categorize the students accurately as to which level of processing they used, solely on the basis of verbal behavior. As to the differences in how the two groups of students processed information, the researchers stated that as the deep-elaborative processors talked about their problems, "they spent more time exploring the meanings of those data rather than simply listing them. In other words, they were more conclusion oriented, attempting to formulate hypotheses about the underlying dynamics or causes of their problems. Their verbalizations were more personalized, that is, related to themselves and containing more clearly defined terms and illustrative examples" (p. 253). The shallow-reiterative processors, in contrast, "were description oriented, spending more time listing details and less time exploring the meanings. Their descriptions were less clear and less personal. In general, they seemed to draw few conclusions or hypotheses from the data" (p. 253).

Communication between counselor and client is enhanced when they have similar cognitive styles (Marshall 1985). In a study of 25 counseling clients from urban areas in eastern Canada, a researcher hypothesized that clients would prefer to have counselors whose approaches in the counseling process corresponded to their own learning styles. Using Kolb's experiential learning cycle as a theoretical base, she stated that the four basic modes corresponded to the four major theoretical counseling approaches: Concrete experience is analogous to the experiential or Gestalt approach, abstract conceptualization to the rational or cognitive approach, active experimentation to the behavioral approach, and reflective observation to the client-centered approach. The results did not confirm the four-way model, but they did give limited support to a two-way model. Clients preferring the client-centered or experiential approaches were more concrete, while clients preferring the behavioral or rational approaches were more abstract.

In another study, Kolb's experiential learning theory was used as a framework for a supervisory course to train counselors to become more sensitive to all modes of experienced-based learning (Abbey, Hunt, and Weiser 1985). The four modes of the cycle were useful in describing the sequences of counseling; variations among clients, counselors, and supervisors; and how the variations affect counseling and supervision.

Clients with a high need for structure respond to the use of formal contracts in counseling that specify desired behavior, expected outcomes, and reward for meeting the specifications of the contract (Griggs 1985). Those with a low need for structure respond well to more open-ended and less well-defined activities and outcomes.

Second, clients who prefer a global mode of processing information are holistic and visual-spatial and profit from such techniques as art therapy, techniques geared to relaxation, meditation, and visual emphases. Those clients who are more analytical respond well to rational-emotive therapy and bibliocounseling. Third, clients prefer either individual or peer counseling. Fourth, clients have varying preferences and strengths in terms of perceptual abilities. Fifth, some clients are highly motivated and enter counseling with enthusiasm and a commitment to change. Clients with low motivation need approaches that emphasize personal involvement, such as game therapy.

In the area of academic advising, a study was conducted to test a comprehensive approach to increasing retention and the academic performance of students enrolled in a high-risk program at a large university (Jenkins and others 1981). The purpose was to "find out the cognitive learning style [that] would appear to work most effectively with the students" (p. 2). Advisers provided the students with a series of tests and academic counseling. Based on the information generated in the testing and advising sessions, they helped the students work on developing the skills necessary to succeed in their courses.

To determine students' cognitive style, researchers used the Prescription for Learning developed by Dixon (n.d.), which considers 52 factors related to learning (including such items as listening, observation, persistence, reading, mobility, noise, and educational values). Based on the inventory, students were able to see which teaching methods and study strategies were probably the most helpful to them. They were thus better able, when they had a choice, to select instructors using what they had learned and, when they had no choice, to adapt to the teacher. After participating in the study for two semesters, the students showed a greater gain on grade point average than those in the control group.

[Students] were thus better able, when they had a choice, to select instructors using what they had learned and, when they had no choice, to adapt to the teacher.

Counselors can use information about learning style to intervene when students are having problems in class. Rockland Community College in Suffern, New York, for example, has an Office of Student Grievances that provides "third-party intervention" when students have difficulty in classes (Claxton, Adams, and Williams 1982, p. 9). In one instance, a student was upset when his English instructor told him to drop the class because of his behavior. The director of the office talked with the instructor and the student about the problem and then administered the Canfield Learning Style Inventory to the student. "The results revealed that his preferred mode of learning was high in small discussion groups, with a high need for knowing the instructor personally, a high need for independence, and a low need for authority. The teaching style of the English instructor was predominantly lecture with minimal discussion, an emphasis on classroom order and strong discipline" (p. 10).

While such findings led to no absolute conclusions, they provided reasonable indications that the student might function better in another classroom. With the director's help, the student transferred to another class in which the instructor taught in ways more congruent with the student's preferred style.

In a related area, counselors and faculty may find information about learning style helpful in dealing with the problem of attrition. Learning style (among other factors) has been studied to develop better ways to predict the academic performance and persistence of community college students (Blustein et al. 1986). Researchers provided a series of tests for 50 students at one college and conducted individual interviews with 30 of them. The testing included the Description Test of Language Skills (College Board 1978), used to measure cognitive ability, the Survey of Study Habits and Attitudes (Brown and Holtzman 1967), the Career Decision Scale (Osipow et al. 1980), the Personality Research Form (Jackson 1974), used to assess students' general motivation, and the Canfield Learning Style Inventory.

Only two variables were significantly related to grade point averages: expectation for learning (from the Canfield instrument), which accounted for 38 percent of the variance, and reading comprehension ability, which accounted for 18 percent of the variance. The score on expectations correlated with three scores on the Survey of Study Habits and Attitudes to provide what the authors refer to as "an attitudinal factor relating to study habits and expectations from learning" (p. 246). This factor, when combined with reading comprehension ability, provided the most powerful predictor of grade point average.

Kolb's model of learning style has been used extensively in career development. The Learning Style Inventory was used, along with other instruments, to investigate the effects of clients' learning style on satisfaction with the System of Interactive Guidance and Instruction (SIGI), the rating of values, and the selection of an occupational field of interest (Pelsma 1984). With SIGI, satisfaction ratings by individuals in each of the four groups of learning styles did not differ significantly; groups did differ, however, on ratings of some values. For instance, convergers rated high income significantly higher than accommodators. Convergers preferred dealing with things rather than people, unlike accommodators, and both assimilators and convergers rated the value of leisure higher than accommodators. Only slight evidence suggested that different groups choose significantly different main occupational fields of interest.

A study of career counselors' learning styles found that a majority of the counselors were characterized by a divergent learning style (Torbit 1981). Lending support to experiential learning theory, this research concluded that individuals are inclined to enter academic and vocational fields consistent with their own learning style.

The concept of learning style and the models of Hill, Canfield, and Kolb have been identified as offering career counselors a helpful "life theme" in working with clients in his or her career search (Gysbers and Moore 1987, pp. 46–50). In fact, Kolb's theory of experiential learning has been suggested as a "meta-model" for career development (Atkinson and Murrell *In press*). The four-step cycle can be helpful in guiding activities designed to facilitate self-exploration and career exploration.

In the first, for example, students could prepare a vocational life history that describes different job experiences (concrete experience), engage in a guided imagery process to promote personal evaluation (reflective observation), take tests like the Strong-Campbell Interest Inventory and have them interpreted by a counselor (abstract conceptualization), and interview personnel directors to explore how they might apply their skills in that particular career (active experimentation).

Similarly, in exploring the world of work, students might spend a day with individuals in different professions to get a first-hand view of those careers (concrete experience), participate in small-group discussion to share reaction to their experiences with the people they visited (reflective observation), attend a lecture on decision-making strategies (abstract conceptualization), and engage in role playing to simulate job interviews or problem situations on the job (active experimentation).

Learning style is a helpful tool in career guidance because "many of the characteristics people prefer in the learning environments correspond to similar characteristics in work environments" (Cafferty 1980, p. 2), and various aspects of Canfield's inventory can be related to the work setting. Under conditions, for example, some workers prefer more than others knowing the instructor (the supervisor) well; under content, some workers may prefer jobs with a numeric orientation or working with numbers and logic (accounting, for example), while others prefer work with a qualitative orientation, such as writing or editing; and under mode, some workers prefer jobs that entail a great deal of reading, while others prefer dealing with information through iconic activities. As to the expectancy part of Canfield's inventory, whether workers expect to do well in their job or are pessimistic about it is an important variable that affects performance and satisfaction.

Thus, "understanding one's own style provides the student with self-knowledge about the kind of environment within which he prefers to interact. Comparing the characteristics of the individual to a complete task analysis of an occupation can provide more complete information on which the student can base his decision on whether to pursue that particular career" (Cafferty 1980, p. 9).

The University of Louisville in Kentucky has a great deal of experience in using Kolb's Learning Style Inventory in student orientation. According to the acting vice president for student affairs, all incoming freshmen take the LSI as part of the summer orientation program.* Members of the faculty, who have received training in use of the instrument, serve as small-group leaders and help students to score the inventory and to understand the results. During this "empowering process," leaders explain that students will be in some courses where the teaching is inconsistent with how they best learn. They then work with the students to identify learning and study strategies they can use in that case. For example, students in a purely lecture course who prefer learning through interaction with peers can make a special effort to locate other students with a similar preference in the class and plan regular small-group study sessions. Thus, students are more likely to be successful in their courses.

The student affairs staff has used the data on learning style to work with a department that had a high dropout rate in its classes, sharing with the department chair the data on learning style for the students who had dropped out and asking the administrator to describe the predominant teaching methods used in the classes. As the discussion went on, it became clear that the approaches to teaching were a striking mismatch for most of the students. The department was then able to address the problem.

The Office of Career and Life Planning at Louisville also conducts workshops on learning style for adults in the area. The sessions serve as a helpful recruitment device, as the participants have an opportunity to get to know members of the faculty and staff. An unexpected payoff occurred when a member of the university's medical school faculty attended a workshop. He liked the Learning Style Inventory so much that he has asked for help in using it with his own students.

Several important points emerge from this discussion. Perhaps most important is that for learning style to have a po-

*Dale Adams 1987, personal communication.

tent effect on an institution, it needs to be a concern not just in the classroom. "All aspects of college—orientation, curriculum, counseling, instruction, and social life—must contribute to both personal empowerment and social perspective" (*Chronicle* 1986, p. 19). For that phenomenon to occur, both faculty and student development personnel need to know about the role learning plays in the development of the student as a whole person and the use of information about learning style in extracurricular life as well as in courses. Developmental theory in general and information about learning style in particular provide a context whereby student development personnel can join the faculty in making a significant contribution to this end.

Second, evidence suggests that matching clients' and counselors' styles can help to promote better communication and the client's comfort. This observation seems particularly important for poorly prepared freshmen and returning adults, many of whom experience considerable anxiety and stress. Counseling situations that put them at ease seem very much in order.

Third, work with Schmeck's model indicates that counselors can identify a client's learning style solely by being trained to be alert to verbal behavior, eliminating the time-consuming and perhaps awkward use of a learning style instrument and enabling the counselor to be more knowledgeable about the kind of structure to provide, the questions to ask, and the activities to have clients engage in.

Fourth, research shows that the Canfield Learning Style Inventory and other instruments are useful in predicting persistence. Data from such instruments can help institutions set up an "early warning system" to identify potential dropouts and provide extra services in counseling, study skills, and individualized teaching.

Fifth, such instruments help students become more knowledgeable about their own preferred ways of learning and help them develop strategies for coping with classes that are difficult for them.

Sixth, three aspects of the experience at Louisville are worth noting—(1) the ability of the student affairs staff to talk to the department chair in very concrete terms about that department's problem with attrition because it had useful, directly relevant data, (2) the student affairs staff's involving faculty members as leaders of the student groups in the summer orientation program, thereby helping faculty to become more sensitive and insightful about learning style, and (3) the provision of opportunities for faculty to learn about their own preferred ways of learning and to make the ideas associated with learning a central ingredient in the institution's ongoing conversation and actions. Thus, learning style and improved teaching become an integral part of a college or university.

Seventh, information about learning style may be very helpful when a student is having problems in a class and counseling is called for. Indeed, it can be argued that counselors can make some of the most important uses of information about learning style. It is they who are trained in the administration and interpretation of tests and who are skilled at intervening in situations involving problems. Thus, student development personnel are particularly well positioned to assist students with problems, and knowledge about learning style may be a very helpful variable in this process. Such a suggestion makes it imperative, however, that preparation programs for student development personnel provide a solid base of understanding of learning style. And developmental theories of human growth should be at the core of such preparation programs (Ivey and Goncalves 1987).

In addition to its usefulness in teaching and student affairs, learning style is relevant for the work setting generally and for administration in higher education in particular. While learning style has been the focus of very little research in this context, what is available in the literature is promising. The topic is important because in the future all organizations will need to be "learning organizations" (Bennis and Nanus 1985, p. 190). To stay alive and vibrant, organizations will increasingly embrace learning as a central issue and act in ways that facilitate it. Because learning style has an important role in effective learning, organizations need to be knowledgeable about it and provide processes and structures that recognize and respond to the individual differences learners bring, including their learning style.

Further, how we work together in the future will be more and more influenced by our particular personality and learning orientation. Several years ago, it was suggested that in the future we will do more and more of our work through "adhocracies," temporary groups formed to accomplish particular tasks (Toffler 1970). While this trend may not have reached full fruition yet, a move is certainly afoot in business and industry toward the use of problem-solving groups where responsibility for tasks is dictated more by who has the requisite skills than by where the person is in the hierarchy. Thus, explicit knowledge and discussion of style will become more important, because they can help us be better informed about people's relative strengths.

Kolb (1976c) used the Learning Style Inventory (1976a) and the experiential learning cycle to conduct research in the work setting and found that managers generally are strong in skills requiring active experimentation but weak in skills requiring reflective observation. Faculty members at business schools in universities tend to have the opposite skills, thus shedding light on the disjuncture between theory and practice that managers and academicians often experience when working together.

Two other studies have examined related issues. The first looked at the relationship between the learning styles of investment portfolio managers in the trust department of a bank and their problem-solving and decision-making skills in managing assets in their portfolios (Stabell 1973). The researcher found that those persons who had high scores on active experimentation and concrete experience tended to be in the investment advisory section, a high-risk, pressure-filled unit. In contrast, those persons with high scores in reflective observation tended to be in the personal trust section, where risk and job pressures were much lower. He further found that managers with an orientation toward concrete experience used people as important sources of information, while managers who were high in abstract conceptualization depended more on printed materials.

The second study examined differences in problem-solving strategies of accommodators and assimilators in a laboratory computer simulation (Grochow 1973). The researcher found that accommodators tended to use approaches that demanded relatively little complexity and changed strategies as they obtained additional data. Assimilators chose more analytical strategies and tended not to change them as the work progressed.

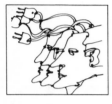

Two conclusions result from such findings. First, learning should be an explicit objective of organizations so that managers and staff can learn from their experiences. Second, opposing perspectives (concrete involvement versus analytical detachment and action versus reflection) should be valued, because all four are needed if learning is to be truly effective (Kolb 1976c).

Persons of different styles can be used to perform particular kinds of responsibilities—divergers for generating ideas and alternatives, assimilators for defining problems and using theory and formulating models, convergers for measuring and evaluating and making decisions, and accommodators for accomplishing tasks and dealing with the people involved in carrying out projects (Hunsaker and Alessandra 1980, pp. 29–30).

In a discussion of management teams in the field of nursing, one researcher suggests that Kolb's Learning Style Inventory can "provide a management team insights into its member or group characteristics [that] might be overlooked or ignored" (Thomas 1986, p. 45). For example:

a nurse-administrator's awareness of learning type could influence decisions in assigning managers and grouping them to carry out management projects and functions more efficiently. Requesting an accommodator to conceive and design a theoretical project, for example, may actually delay getting that job done effectively. On the other hand, the assimilator on the team may seize upon such an assignment enthusiastically. The converger may not be inclined to brainstorm ideas solving a given problem as well as the diverger who is delighted to contribute (p. 47).

A questionnaire can help identify different styles in the work setting: *activists*, who are action oriented and creative but less interested in implementation and consolidation; *reflectors*, who prefer to stand back and ponder experiences cautiously; *theorists*, who are skilled in adapting and integrating observations into complex but sound theories; and *pragmatists*, who are good at trying out new ideas to see whether they work in practice (Honey and Mumford 1986).

Some tasks are most appropriately carried out by groups comprised of people with varied styles. For example, a heterogeneous group might be used to solve a complex problem, with each person bringing his or her own strengths to the situation. In such cases, it is probably helpful if the members are knowledgeable about styles and sensitive to the perspectives of each person. This kind of group, especially when informed of each other's style, is "better at achieving set objectives [and will] produce higher quality work, meet deadlines more comfortably, and interact more efficiently with less interrupting, more listening, more building..." (p. 70).

Conversely, some tasks might be more appropriate for a homogeneous group. Once a problem has been solved and implementation has been agreed upon, a group of persons with common styles might be better at carrying out the plan.

Administrators who use style in assigning tasks should be careful not to ignore the realities of the reward system in a given work setting. To use a person's strengths to perform tasks that are not valued not only takes unfair advantage of that person but also denies him or her opportunities to develop competence in using other styles.

No literature is available that provides models or theoretical frameworks for guiding administrators where learning style—in teaching and in work arrangements—is a major concern. Suggestions have been made, however, for administrative practices in institutions where student development is the explicit purpose. If a college is committed to student development, "a similar concern for the developmental needs of the faculty should be embraced as a central concern of the institution" (Claxton and Murrell 1984, p. 42). This concern can be operationalized in such areas as faculty planning and evaluation, tenure and promotion, and professional development. A fundamental principle is to affirm the strengths professors bring, help them find ways to strengthen other capacities, and work together toward the achievement of the institution's mission.

Leaders of true learning organizations face special challenges.

The effective administrative leader is one who will be sensitive to the developmental issues being addressed by faculty members, utilize the energy generated through the resolution of those issues, and provide them with the nurturance, support, and encouragement they will need in a climate that values the developmental process. Such an institutional stance of generativity can only be created by administrators who are aware of and working on their own personal growth and development (Claxton and Murrell 1984, p. 43).

RELATED ISSUES

Several questions cut across all the models of learning style that have important implications for teaching, student affairs, and the work setting: (1) Are the learning styles of minority students different from those of students of the dominant culture? (2) How can learning style be defined? (3) How adequate is current instrumentation to measure learning style? (4) What are the advantages of matching versus mismatching?

Very little research has been done on the learning style of minority students in higher education, but an examination of the influence of Afro-American culture on child rearing is instructive because "we must understand the culture of black children if we are to gain insight into their learning styles" (Hale-Benson 1982, p. 4). Drawing on the work of Cohen (1969), who identifies two styles of learning (*analytical*, which is parts specific and objective and views information as it is rather than in its context, and *relational*, which is global and subjective and views information in its own context), Hale-Benson notes that schools focus almost entirely on the analytic approach to learning. Thus, children "who have not developed these skills and those who function with a different cognitive style will not only be poor achievers early in school, but [will]...also become worse as they move to higher grade levels" (p. 31). Schools in the United States orient their curricula to the analytical style, but "black people and lower-income people tend to utilize a predominantly relational style" (p. 37). The recommendation, aimed at early childhood education, is a balanced curriculum "so that Afro-American culture (with its emphasis on high affective support and creative expression) is explored and legitimated at the same time the children are taught about Euro-American and other cultures" (pp. 160–61).

The conclusion that black children are oriented primarily to a relational learning style is tentative and needs to be the focus of further empirical research. Nevertheless, these findings clearly have significant implications for teaching black students in colleges and universities. The idea of two predominant styles, one analytic and one relational, is consistent with the model of splitters and lumpers. The need for curricular experiences anchored in both is obvious.

Another study investigated the learning styles of Native American students in a community college biology course, with a view toward changing teaching-learning processes and suggesting improved curriculum development in science (Haukoos and Satterfield 1986). The study gathered data on 20 na-

The conclusion that black children are oriented primarily to a relational learning style is tentative and needs to be the focus of further empirical research.

tive students and 20 nonnative students; the groups were nearly identical in age, educational background, and other variables but differed in race, culture, and socioeconomic status.

The results of the learning style inventory administered to the students showed that the native students were more visual linguistic than auditory linguistic and preferred not to express themselves orally. The nonnative students were more auditory and numerical linguistic than visual linguistic and preferred to express themselves orally.

To respond to the high visual-perceptive and low verbal and expressive skills exhibited in this study, several changes were made in the course for the Native American students: a greater emphasis on discussion than on lectures; more time for students' responses to questions; discussions enriched with slides, graphics, and natural settings; and small-group study. These changes resulted in a climate that was congruent with students' learning styles, and "student success was remarkable" (p. 199). Besides the gain in group dynamics and in interpersonal comfort, the course completion rate increased, and students transferred to senior institutions where they majored in nursing and premedicine.

Yet another study reports research findings on other minority elementary and secondary students (Gardner 1980). Many Native American children are primarily visually oriented and excel in visually related skills like penmanship, spelling, and art. Thus, they are at a disadvantage in typical classrooms where verbal skills, class discussions, and question-and-answer sessions are emphasized. They are more used to learning through observation, through practice that is carefully directed by an adult, and through imitation. They typically resist competition and emphasize cooperation in learning.

Further, Chicano children have been socialized in a culture that emphasizes cooperative and peer interaction rather than individualistic competition, and thus many of them are motivated more by social reinforcement and by helping others. Studies of Japanese and Chinese children show they tend to be able to respond quickly and accurately on timed tests, although a study of Chinese children shows they prefer extra time for reflection before answering. Vietnamese children are used to a traditional educational system that emphasizes rote learning, memorization, repetition, and recollection. (One must note, however, that some of these findings are based on limited studies, and caution is to be used in generalizing to all children of a particular culture.)

The research on learning style, almost without exception, has been done from a Western, white, middle-class perspective and value system. As our culture becomes more pluralistic, higher education will have to face squarely its shortcomings in dealing adequately with its diverse clientele. Because the purpose of studying learning style is to acknowledge and understand individual differences, the cultural antecedents of style will have to be addressed. Research in this area is thus a major priority for the future.

The second issue is definition of learning style. It is clear from this presentation of selected models that the term is used in many different ways: "Cognitive style," for example, has been defined as "cognitive characteristic modes of functioning that we reveal through our perceptual and intellectual activities in a highly consistent and pervasive way" (Witkin 1976, p. 39); as "a superordinate construct...involved in many cognitive operations [that] accounts for individual differences in a variety of cognitive, perceptual, and personality variables" (Vernon 1973, p. 141); and as something that represents "a person's typical modes of perceiving, remembering, thinking, and problem solving (Messick 1970, p. 188).

The term "learning style" came into use when researchers "began to look for specific strategies for combining course presentation and materials to match the particular needs of each learner" (Kirby 1979, p. 35). In this view, then, learning style is a broader term that includes cognitive style. The more inclusive term is useful, although it loses some of the specificity and precision that definitions of cognitive style possessed. Learning style has also been referred to as "a student's consistent way of responding to and using stimuli in the context of learning" (Claxton and Ralston 1978, p. 7), and in a widely accepted definition that is more specific, the term refers to "characteristic cognitive, affective, and physiological behaviors that serve as relatively stable indicators of how learners perceive, interact with, and respond to the learning environment" (Keefe 1979, p. 4).

It is doubtful that any final agreement can be reached on the term until further research has resulted in a more refined theoretical base. Thus, it is important for researchers and practitioners alike to be clear about what aspect of learning preference they are referring to when they use the term.

The third issue is instrumentation. Although "learning style diagnosis gives the most powerful leverage yet available to educators to analyze, motivate, and assist students," measurement of learning style remains problematic (Keefe 1979, p. 132). Practically all of the learning style instruments "rely on rankings and ratings of things important to learners," and thus many of the instruments are "grounded more in attitudes than in behavior" (Grasha 1984, p. 50). With most of the instruments currently in use, it is left to students to decide what the frame of reference is when responding to the inventory (for example, do they respond based on how they act in a particular class or how they see themselves when they are learning on the job?). Further, the reliability and validity of the instruments are low to moderate, and thus a teacher cannot have full faith in the results. And it is often difficult to design a course based on the individual or group data generated by the instruments (pp. 50–51).

A learning style instrument should, however, be able to "demonstrate internal consistency and test-retest reliability, exhibit construct and predictive validity, provide data that can be translated into instructional practices, provide high degrees of satisfaction among learners placed in environments designed on the basis of the information it provided, help facilitate the learners' ability to acquire content and to demonstrate their ability to use content, and perform...in ways that are clearly superior to those without it" (p. 47).

That, it seems, is the challenge for research on measurement of learning style in the future. At the same time, however, the present state of knowledge can clearly be helpful in enhancing educational practices, particularly in terms of helping students learn how to learn and helping faculty become more sensitive to differences in learning style in the classroom. Research and practice must move ahead in tandem in ways that inform each other.

The final issue is matching versus mismatching. How much difference does it make that a student's learning style differs from the instructional method used by the teacher? Is it enough to compel the teacher to focus on learning style rather than other important variables? Present research does not provide clear answers to these questions, but the literature seems to indicate that the assumption of early years was that the task was to identify a student's style and then provide instruction consistent with that style so the student could learn more efficiently.

Strong arguments can be made against such an approach (Doyle and Rutherford 1984). Based on efforts to match instructional method and students' style in the primary and secondary grades, "no single dimension of learners...unambiguously dictates an instructional prescription. Thus, accommodating cognitive style, which is likely to influence motivation primarily, does not necessarily account for other critical variables in learning, such as ability and prior knowledge" (p. 22).

Similar concerns have been raised about matching in higher education (Grasha 1984). At this point, no certainty exists about which learning style variables are the ones most useful in designing instructional processes. Thus, the question of just how important learning style is needs to be addressed through research characterized by sound methodology and improved instrumentation.

Furthermore, the very important question of outcomes—that is, what outcomes are desired for students and what information about learning style is needed in designing instruction to reach the desired outcomes?—is critical. It is why this discussion has been cast in terms of individual development as the central purpose of higher education and why the authors have tried to be particularly attentive to ways human development theory relates to the research findings on learning style. Matching is a means to an instrumental end and can be fully appropriate: Such an approach seems particularly important with poorly prepared students. They very much need to develop the skills necessary for success in college as well as the affirmation such success brings.

At the same time, discontinuity in learning experiences helps students move to new ways of thinking and to develop additional skills for lifelong learning. Experiences that are inconsistent with students' styles can "stretch" students and help them develop new learning skills and aspects of the self necessary for healthy adult functioning. Research that provides the links between style, motivation, and development is critical in the years ahead so that matching and mismatching can be done systematically and in an informed way.

An elusive connection spoken to in this discussion is the relationship of learning style to developmental stage and to disciplinary perspectives. What are the links between style and epistemologies, or ways of knowing?

A study of 135 women representing all socioeconomic groups concerning how they view themselves, authority, and

knowledge describes two different epistemologies—"separate knowing," which is clearly dominant in higher education, and "connected knowing," which is rarely honored in the academy (Belenky et al. 1986). Separate knowing emphasizes objectivity, detachment, and rational thinking, while connected knowing emphasizes subjectivity, involvement, and intuition. The effects of the dominant epistemology on women can be seen in a number of teaching practices, according to the authors. Women in the study who had been to college reported that they were frequently told their personal experience could be expected to be a source of error, clearly implying that experience is not as valuable as more objective rational ways of knowing. The authors suggest that female students can profit from starting not with what the professor knows but with their own experience and what they know.

Other important differences occur between separate knowing and connected knowing. In separate knowing is an emphasis on doubting and skepticism, while persons who rely more on connected knowing are more oriented to empathy, to finding the aspects of an idea that are true and then building on them. When professors push students to shoot holes in an argument and find its flaws, they are asking women to act in ways inconsistent with their way of orienting themselves to the world.

Professors tend to develop their ideas privately, integrating major research findings, and then reporting the results in lectures or in print in the objective terms of the discipline. But persons oriented toward connected knowing are more comfortable working together in a dialogue to search for a communal, rather than an individual, truth. This emphasis on emerging rather than fully formed ideas places the professor in the role of a resource person who not only provides expert information but also helps students see the issues and construct their world in more complex, more inclusive ways.

The issue of how we know is a fundamental one not simply because it can inform teaching practices but also because "our basic assumptions about the nature of truth and reality and the origins of knowledge shape the way we see the world and ourselves as participants in it" (Belenky et al. 1986, p. 3). This view closely parallels another:

> I do not believe that epistemology is a bloodless abstraction; the way we know has powerful implications for the way we live...Every epistemology tends to become an ethic,

and...every way of knowing tends to become a way of liv-
ing...The relation established between the knower and the
known, between the student and the subject, tends to become
the relation of the living person to the world itself...Every
mode of knowing contains its own moral trajectory, its own
ethical direction and outcomes (Palmer 1987, p. 22).

The two ways of knowing can be related to the issue of community, defined as "a capacity for relatedness" (Palmer 1987,
p. 24). The dominant epistemology of higher education is "objectivism" (p. 22), a description that resonates with separate
knowing. Objectivism distances the knower from the known to
avoid subjectivity. Through this emphasis on objectivity, it
makes what is to be known an object, thereby enabling one to
dissect it and to analyze it to see what makes it tick. Further,
this mode of knowing is experimental in that one can then
move the pieces around in ways that make more sense. The result is that "this seemingly bloodless epistemology...becomes
an ethic...of competitive individualism, in the midst of a world
fragmented and made exploitable by that very mode of knowing" (p. 22).

Thus, objectivism by its very nature is anticommunal. Higher
education needs to move away from its competitive individualism and toward a greater sense of community, but we will
never be able to promote community in higher education, with
the resulting impact on our graduates and the society at large,
as long as we rely only on an objectivist way of knowing (Palmer 1987).

Separate knowing and connected knowing are not gender
specific, although more men probably rely on separate knowing
and more women on connected knowing (Belenky et al. 1986).
Neither Belenky et al. nor Palmer urge that the dominant
epistemology in higher education be replaced by the other.
Rather, both separate knowing and connected knowing need to
be honored, and faculty must help students deal with the creative tension that comes when the two are used in tandem.

These two epistemologies are clearly reminiscent of the two
fundamental orientations that Kirby, Hale-Benson, and others
have identified. Splitters, field independents, serialists, and abstract, analytical learners are more in the objectivist mode of
knowing, and lumpers, field sensitives, holists, and concrete
learners are more in the relational mode. Thus, it appears a major stream of research on learning styles deals in one way or

another with learners' preferences for one of the two ways of knowing.

A distinction has been made between epistemology and style with the two-dimensional model described earlier (Kolb 1984, pp. 99–131). Kolb posits a grasping or prehending dimension of learning in which the learner takes in experience concretely or abstractly, analogous to the two epistemologies discussed earlier. A second step in learning is transforming reflectively or actively the experience one has taken in. It is the two together, the prehending dimension and the transforming dimension, that in Kolb's view is learning style.

Further research and theory are needed to delineate the dynamics of style, epistemology, developmental stage, and disciplinary perspective. What is clear already is that teaching practices are needed that honor both analytic and relational knowing. If Palmer is correct in his thesis that every way of knowing becomes a way of living, it is imperative that faculty help students learn in ways that help them develop skill in both. By honoring both analytical and relational ways of knowing, we may make our greatest contribution—not only to effective learning but also to building a greater sense of community as well.

CONCLUSIONS AND RECOMMENDATIONS FOR ACTION

Learning style is a concept that can play an important role in improving teaching and learning practices in higher education. Researchers have defined the term in various ways, which may be ordered in terms of students' preferences or orientations at four levels: personality, information processing, social interaction, and instructional methods.

Having information on style can help faculty become more sensitive to the differences students bring to the classroom. It can also serve as a guide to the design of learning experiences that match or mismatch students' style, depending on whether the purpose of the experience is instrumental or developmental. From students' perspective, evidence indicates that learning about their own style increases their chances of succeeding in courses. At the same time, activities that help them develop strategies for learning in ways other than their predominant style are important. This experience of learning how to learn is an empowering one that can help students become successful lifelong learners.

Information about learning style can be helpful in student affairs in counseling, career development, advising, and orientation. It can be useful in the work setting to inform efforts to deploy staff members in ways that call on their major strengths. At the same time, it is important that faculty and staff have opportunities to develop in areas other than in their predominant style as well. A college or university that is seriously interested in development of students as a purpose needs to embrace such a concept for faculty and administrators as well.

Institutions interested in making learning style an important part of the teaching-learning process may wish to consider the following recommendations for actions:

1. *Conduct professional development activities on the use of learning style in improving teaching and student development.*

Workshops, seminars, the use of minigrants for instructional improvement projects, and similar activities can be useful in helping participants better understand the importance of style and its role in improving students' learning. Planners should be especially careful to ensure that the activities, such as workshops, exemplify the teaching principles espoused therein.

2. *Promote classroom research and make data about learning style an important part of it.*

Classroom research can be an important strategy in bringing some balance to the way many institutions prize research and undervalue teaching (Cross 1987). The definition of research

This experience of learning how to learn is an empowering one that can help students become successful lifelong learners.

could be broadened to include not only research in the specialized disciplines but also in teaching-learning processes. Information on style, when linked with other data on students, holds great promise for helping faculty members improve their teaching. The collection and use of such data can also contribute to a continuing dialogue among faculty and administrators as they learn from each other about teaching and learning.

3. *Establish curricular experiences that focus on helping students learn how to learn.*

Orientation activities or a credit-bearing course ("An Introduction to College") can be geared to helping students better understand how learning occurs and the role of the disciplines in the development of thinking skills. Learning style inventories and other processes can be used to help make them aware of their own preferences and strengths. Attention should also be given to helping students develop strategies for succeeding in courses taught in ways that are incongruent with their primary learning abilities.

4. *In hiring new faculty members, take into account candidates' understanding of teaching-learning practices that recognize individual differences, including style.*

In the next 10 to 20 years, colleges and universities will hire thousands of new faculty members to replace those who will be retiring or leaving the field of higher education. In the past, the Ph.D., with its emphasis on specialized study in the discipline and its predominant orientation to research, was taken as the necessary credential for teaching. Today, with an increasingly diverse student body and research that clearly identifies the elements of effective college teaching (Cross 1987), a greater realization exists that faculty preparation should include other areas of knowledge as well. Research in student development, learning theory, and ways to use the creative tension between content and process are all important prerequisites for effective teaching. Administrative leaders have the opportunity to make a major contribution to improved learning by hiring faculty with such preparation.

Beyond steps colleges and universities should take to use theory of learning style is an important research agenda that needs to be carried out as well. The most pressing need is to learn more about the learning preferences of minority students. This void in the literature is particularly serious in light of the increasing numbers of minority and international students higher education will serve.

Second, more research is needed that clarifies how much difference it makes if teaching methods are incongruent with students' style. Studies that speak to the role and potency of style, seen in conjunction with other important variables, would help teachers significantly. The development of better instrumentation to identify style should be a key part of such research.

Third, research is needed that illuminates the connections and interaction between style, developmental stage, disciplinary perspectives, and epistemology. A better understanding of those links would be a helpful framework for examining teaching methodologies, the role of learning in individual development, and the use of the disciplines to promote more complex and integrative ways of thinking.

REFERENCES

The Educational Resources Information Center (ERIC) Clearinghouse
on Higher Education abstracts and indexes the current literature on
higher education for inclusion in ERIC's data base and announcement
in ERIC's monthly bibliographic journal, *Resources in Education*
(RIE). Most of these publications are available through the ERIC Document Reproduction Service (EDRS). For publications cited in this
bibliography that are available from EDRS, ordering number and price
are included. Readers who wish to order a publication should write to
the ERIC Document Reproduction Service, 3900 Wheeler Avenue,
Alexandria, Virginia 22304. (Phone orders with VISA or MasterCard
are taken at 800/227-ERIC or 703/823-0500.) When ordering, please
specify the document (ED) number. Documents are available as noted
in microfiche (MF) and paper copy (PC). Because prices are subject
to change, it is advisable to check the latest issue of *Resources in
Education* for current cost based on the number of pages in the
publication.

Abbey, D.S.; Hunt, D.E.; and Weiser, J.C. 1985. "Variations on a
Theme by Kolb: A New Perspective for Understanding Counseling
and Supervision." *The Counseling Psychologist* 13: 477–501.

Abraham, Roberta. December 1985. "Field Independence-Dependence
and the Teaching of Grammar." *TESOL Quarterly* 20: 689–702.

Adams, V.M., and McLeod, D.B. November 1979. "The Interaction
of Field Dependence/Independence and the Level of Guidance of
Mathematics Instruction." *Journal for Research in Mathematics Education* 10: 347–55.

Allport, Gordon. 1961. *Pattern and Growth in Personality*. New
York: Holt, Rinehart & Winston.

Alpert, R., and Haber, R. 1960. "Anxiety in Academic Achievement
Situations." *Journal of Abnormal and Social Psychology* 61:
207–15.

Andrews, John D.W. March 1981. "Teaching Format and Students'
Style: Their Interactive Effects on Learning." *Research in Higher
Education* 14: 161–78.

Ashcroft, Barbara. 1986. "Predictive Validity of the Canfield
Learning Style Inventory for Determining Persistence in an Under-
graduate Engineering Program." Doctoral dissertation, Memphis
State University.

Atkinson, George, and Murrell, Patricia. *In press*. "Kolb's Experiential Learning Theory: A Meta-Model for Career Exploration." *Journal of Counseling and Development.*

Ausubel, D.P. 1963. *The Psychology of Meaningful Verbal Learning*.
New York: Grune & Stratton.

Babich, A., and Randol, P. 1976. *Learning Styles Inventory Report*.
Wichita, Kan.: Murdock Teaching Center.

Ballard, F.B. 1980. "The Effect of Leadership Styles and Learning

Styles on Student Achievement in a Basic Business Course at Florida Junior College at Jacksonville." Doctoral dissertation, Florida State University.

Belenky, M.F.; Clinchy, B.M.; Goldberger, N.R.; and Tarule, J.M. 1986. *Women's Ways of Knowing: The Development of Self, Voice, and Mind*. New York: Basic Books.

Bennis, Warren, and Nanus, Burt. 1985. *Leaders: Strategies for Taking Charge*. New York: Harper & Row.

Blustein, D.; Judd, T.; Krom, J.; Viniar, B.; Padilla, E.; Wedemeyer, R.; and Williams, D. May 1986. "Identifying Predictors of Academic Performance of Community College Students." *Journal of College Student Personnel* 27: 242–49.

Brillhart, Lia V. February 1981. "Responsive Education Applied to Engineering Mechanics." *Engineering Education* 71: 345–49.

Brillhart, L., and Debs, M.B. Spring 1982. "An Engineering-Rhetoric Course: Combining Learning-Teaching Styles." *Improving College and University Teaching* 30: 80–85.

Brown, W., and Holtzman, W. 1967. *Survey of Study Habits and Attitudes Manual*. New York: Psychological Corporation.

Bruffee, Kenneth A. March/April 1987. "The Art of Collaborative Learning." *Change* 19: 42–47.

Butler, Kathleen. 1984. *Learning and Teaching Style in Theory and Practice*. Maynard, Mass.: Gabriel Systems.

Cafferty, E. 1980. "Learning Style as a Tool in Career Guidance." Paper presented at the annual meeting of the American Vocational Association, New Orleans, Louisiana, 6 December. ED 195 709. 12 pp. MF–$1.04; PC–$3.85.

Canfield, Albert. 1980. *Learning Styles Inventory Manual*. Ann Arbor, Mich.: Humanics Media.

Canfield, Albert, and Canfield, Judith S. 1986. *Canfield Instructional Styles Inventory*. Ann Arbor, Mich.: Humanics Media.

Certo, S.C., and Lamb, S.W. 1980. "An Investigation of Bias with the Learning Style Inventory through Factor Analysis." *Journal of Experiential Learning and Simulation* 2: 1–7.

Chickering, A.W., and associates. 1981. *The Modern American College*. San Francisco: Jossey-Bass.

Chickering, A.W., and Havighurst, Robert J. 1981. "The Life Cycle." In *The Modern American College*, by A.W. Chickering and associates. San Francisco: Jossey-Bass.

Chronicle of Higher Education. 5 November 1986. "Prologue and Major Recommendations of Carnegie Foundation's Report on Colleges": 16.

Claxton, Charles; Adams, Dale; and Williams, Dell. May 1982. "Using Student Learning Styles in Teaching." *AAHE Bulletin* 34: 7–10.

Claxton, Charles, and Murrell, Patricia. 1984. "Developmental
Theory as a Guide for Maintaining the Vitality of College Faculty."
In *Teaching and Aging*, edited by C.M.N. Mehrotra. New Direc-
tions for Teaching and Learning No. 19. San Francisco: Jossey-
Bass.

Claxton, Charles, and Ralston, Yvonne. 1978. *Learning Styles: Their
Impact on Teaching and Administration*. AAHE-ERIC Higher Edu-
cation Report No. 10. Washington, D.C.: American Association for
Higher Education. ED 167 065. 74 pp. MF–$1.04; PC–$7.76.

Cohen, Rosalie. 1969. "Conceptual Styles, Culture Conflict, and
Nonverbal Tests of Intelligence." *American Anthropologist* 71:
828–56.

College Board. 1978. *Descriptive Tests of Language Skills*. Princeton,
N.J.: Educational Testing Service.

Cross, K. Patricia. September 1986. "A Proposal to Improve Teaching." *AAHE Bulletin* 19: 9–14. ED 274 257. 7 pp. MF–$1.04; PC–
$3.85.

———. March 1987. "The Adventures of Education in Wonderland:
Implementing Education Reform." *Phi Delta Kappan* 68: 496–502.

Curry L. 1983. "An Organization of Learning Styles Theory and Con-
structs." Paper presented at the annual meeting of the American
Educational Research Association, Montreal, Quebec, 11–15 April.
ED 235 185. 28 pp. MF–$1.04; PC–$5.82.

Daloz, Laurent. 1986. *Effective Teaching and Mentoring: Realizing
the Transformational Power of Adult Learning Experiences*. San
Francisco: Jossey-Bass.

Dewey, J. 1938. *Experience and Education*. New York: McMillan &
Co.

Dixon, Nancy. n.d. "Prescription for Learning Test Booklet." Austin,
Tex.: Department of Curriculum and Instruction.

———. July 1982. "Incorporating Learning Style into Training
Design." *Training and Development Journal* 36: 62–64.

Doyle, W., and Rutherford, B. Winter 1984. "Classroom Research on
Matching Learning and Teaching Styles." *Theory into Practice* 23:
20–24.

Dunn, Rita; Dunn, Kenneth; and Price, G.E. 1978. *Learning Style
Inventory Manual*. Lawrence, Kan.: Price Systems.

———. 1982. *Productivity: Environmental Preference Survey
Manual*. Lawrence, Kan.: Price Systems.

Education Commission of the States. 30 July 1986. "Transforming the
State Role in Undergraduate Education." *Chronicle of Higher
Education*: 13–18.

Ehrhardt, H. August 1983. "Utilization of Cognitive Style in the
Clinical Laboratory Sciences." *American Journal of Medical Technology* 49: 569–77.

Eison, J. 1979. "The Development and Validation of a Scale to Assess Differing Learning Orientations toward Grades and Learning." Doctoral dissertation, University of Tennessee.

Eison, J., and Moore, J. 1980. "Learning Styles and Attitudes of Traditional Age and Adult Students." Paper presented at the 88th Annual Convention of the American Psychological Association, Montreal, Quebec, September.

Fizzell, R. Spring 1984. "The Status of Learning Styles." *The Educational Forum*: 303–11.

Flippo, R.F., and Terrell, W.R. May 1984. "Personalized Instruction: An Exploration of Its Effects on Developmental Reading Students' Attitudes and Self-Confidence." *Reading World* 23: 315–24.

Ford, Nigel. June 1985. "Styles and Strategies of Processing Information: Implications for Professional Education." *Education for Information* 3: 115–32.

Fourier, M.J. 1980. "The Effectiveness of Disclosure of Students' Educational Cognitive Style Maps on Academic Achievement in Selected Community College Courses." Doctoral dissertation, University of Missouri.

Fox, Robert D. Winter 1984. "Learning Styles and Instructional Preferences in Continuing Education for Health Professionals: A Validity Study of the LSI." *Adult Education Quarterly* 35: 72–85.

Freedman, R.D., and Stumpf, S.A. 1978. "What Can One Learn from the Learning Style Inventory?" *Academy of Management Journal* 21: 275–82.

———. 1980. "Learning Style Theory: Less than Meets the Eye." *Academy of Management Review* 5: 445–47.

Fuhrmann, Barbara, and Grasha, Anthony. 1983. *Designing Classroom Experiences Based on Student Styles and Teaching Styles: A Practical Handbook for College Teaching.* Boston: Little, Brown & Co.

Gardner, R. 1980. "Learning Styles: What Every Teacher Should Consider." Paper presented at the Rocky Mountain Regional Conference of the International Reading Association, Boise, Idaho, 1 November. ED 198 059. 10 pp. MF–$1.04; PC–$3.85.

Gibbs, G. 1977. "Can Students Be Taught How to Study?" *Higher Education Bulletin* 5: 107–18.

Grasha, Anthony. February 1972. "Observations on Relating Teaching Goals to Student Response Style and Classroom Methods." *American Psychologist* 27: 144–47.

———. Winter 1984. "Learning Styles: The Journey from Greenwich Observatory (1796) to the College Classroom (1984)." *Improving College and University Teaching* 22: 46–53.

Gregorc, A.R. 1979. "Learning/Teaching Styles." In *Student Learning Styles: Diagnosing and Prescribing Programs,* edited by

J.W. Keefe. Reston, Va.: National Association of Secondary School Principals.

Gregorc, A.R., and Ward, H.G. 1977. "Implications for Learning and Teaching: A New Definition for Individuals." *NASSP Bulletin* 61: 20–23.

Griggs, S.A. November 1985. "Counseling for Individual Learning Styles." *Journal of Counseling and Development* 64: 202–5.

Grochow, J. 1973. "Cognitive Style as a Factor in the Design of Interactive Decision-Support Systems." Doctoral dissertation, Massachusetts Institute of Technology.

Guild, P.B., and Garger, S. 1985. *Marching to Different Drummers.* Alexandria, Va.: Association for Supervision and Curriculum Development.

Gysbers, Norman C., and Moore, Earl J. 1987. *Career Counseling: Skills and Techniques for Practitioners.* Englewood Cliffs, N.J.: Prentice-Hall.

Hale-Benson, Janice E. 1982. *Black Children: Their Roots, Culture, and Learning Styles.* Baltimore: Johns Hopkins University Press.

Haukoos, Gerry, and Satterfield, R. 1986. "Learning Styles of Minority Students (Native Americans) and Their Application in Developing a Culturally Sensitive Science Classroom." *Community/Junior College Quarterly* 10: 193–201.

Hendricson, W.; Berlocher, W.; and Herbert, R. April 1987. "A Four-Year Longitudinal Study of Dental Student Learning Styles." *Journal of Dental Education* 51: 175–81.

Henson, K., and Borthwick, P. Winter 1984. "Matching Styles: A Historical Look." *Theory to Practice* 23: 3–8.

Hill, J.E., and Nunnery, D.N. 1973. *The Educational Sciences.* Bloomfield Hills, Mich.: Oakland Community College Press.

Hodgkinson, H.L. 1985. *All One System: Demographics of Education, Kindergarten through Graduate School.* Washington, D.C.: Institute of Educational Leadership. ED 261 101. 22 pp. MF–$1.04; PC not available EDRS.

Holland, John L. 1966. *The Psychology of Vocational Choice.* Waltham, Mass.: Ginn & Co.

Honey, P., and Mumford, A. 1986. *The Manual of Learning Styles.* Maidenhead, Eng.: Ardingly House.

Hunsaker, P., and Alessandra, A. 1980. *The Art of Managing People.* Englewood Cliffs, N.J.: Prentice-Hall.

Ivey, Allen E., and Goncalves, Oscar F. June 1987. "Toward a Developmental Counseling Curriculum." *Counselor Education and Supervision* 26: 270–78.

Jackson, D.N. 1974. *Personality Research Form—Form E.* Goshen, N.Y.: Educational Testing Service.

Jackson, O.N. 1971. "The Dynamics of Structured Personality Tests: 1971." *Psychological Review* 78: 229–43.

Jenkins, J., and others. 1981. "Promoting Persistence through Cognitive Style Analysis and Self-Management Techniques." Carbondale, Ill.: Southern Illinois University. ED 222 142. 67 pp. MF–$1.04; PC–$7.76.

Kagan, Jerome. 1965. "Reflection Impulsivity and Reading Ability in Primary Grade Children." *Child Development* 36: 609–28.

Katz, Joseph, and Henry, Mildred. *Forthcoming. Turning Professors into Teachers: A New Approach to Faculty Development and Student Learning.* New York: Macmillan.

Keefe, James W. 1979. "Learning Style: An Overview." In *Student Learning Styles: Diagnosing and Prescribing Programs*, edited by J.W. Keefe. Reston, Va.: National Association of Secondary School Principals.

Kegan, Robert. 1982. *The Evolving Self: Problem and Process in Human Development.* Cambridge, Mass.: Harvard University Press.

Kirby, P. 1979. *Cognitive Style, Learning Style, and Transfer Skill Acquisition.* Information Series No. 195. Columbus: Ohio State University, National Center for Research in Vocational Education.

Klein, G. 1951. "The Perceptual World through Perception." In *Perception: An Approach to Personality*, edited by Robert R. Blake and Glenn V. Ramsey. New York: Ronald Press.

Knefelkamp, Lee, and Cornfeld, Janet. 1979. "Combining Student Stage and Style in the Design of Learning Environments: Using Holland Typologies and Perry Stages." Paper presented at a meeting of the American College Personnel Association, Los Angeles, California, March.

Kolb, David A. 1976a. *Learning Style Inventory.* Boston: McBer & Co.

———. 1976b. *Learning Style Inventory Technical Manual.* Boston: McBer & Co.

———. 1976c. "Management and the Learning Process." *California Management Review* 18: 21–31.

———. 1981a. "Experiential Learning Theory and the Learning Style Inventory: A Reply to Freedman and Stumpf." *Academy of Management Review* 6: 289–96.

———. 1981b. "Learning Styles and Disciplinary Differences." In *The Modern American College*, edited by A.W. Chickering and associates. San Francisco: Jossey-Bass.

———. 1984. *Experiential Learning: Experience as the Source of Learning and Development.* New York: Prentice-Hall.

———. 1985. *Learning Style Inventory.* Boston: McBer & Co.

Lassan, R. 1984. "Learning Style Differences: Registered Nurse Students vs. Generic Student Nurses at the Baccalaureate Level." Providence, R.I.: Rhode Island College, Department of Nursing. ED 240 318. 29 pp. MF–$1.04; PC–$5.82.

Lawrence, Gordon. 1982. *People Types and Tiger Stripes: A Practical Guide to Learning Styles.* Gainesville, Fla.: Center for the Application of Psychological Type.

———. 1984. "A Synthesis of Learning Style Research Involving the MBTI." *Journal of Psychological Type* 8: 2–15.

Leonard, A., and Harris, I. 1979. "Learning Style in a Primary Care Internal Medicine Residency Program." *Archives of Internal Medicine* 139: 872–75.

Lewin, K. 1951. *Field Theory in Social Sciences.* San Francisco: Jossey-Bass.

Loevinger, J. 1976. *Ego Development.* San Francisco: Jossey-Bass.

McCart, C.L.; Toombs, W.; Lindsay, C.; and Crowe, M.B. 1985. "Learning Styles among Established Professionals." Paper presented at the annual meeting of the American Educational Research Association, Chicago, Illinois, April. ED 261 086. 31 pp. MF–$1.04; PC–$5.82.

McCarthy, Bernice. 1981. *The 4Mat System: Teaching to Learning Styles with Right/Left Mode Techniques.* Oak Brook, Ill.: EXCEL, Inc.

McCarthy, Patricia; Shaw, T.; and Schmeck, R. 1986. "Behavioral Analysis of Client Learning Style during Counseling." *Journal of Counseling Psychology* 33: 249–54.

McCaulley, Mary H., and Natter, Frank L. 1980. *Psychological (Myers-Briggs) Type Differences in Education.* Gainesville, Fla.: Center for the Application of Psychological Type.

McDade, C. April 1978. "Subsumption versus Educational Set: Implications for Sequencing of Instructional Materials." *Journal of Educational Psychology* 70: 137–41.

McMullan, W., and Cahoon, A. 1979. "Integrating Abstract Conceptualization with Experiential Learning." *Academy of Management Review* 4: 453–58.

Macneil, R. July/August 1980. "The Relationship of Cognitive Style and Instructional Style to the Learning Performance of Undergraduate Students." *Journal of Educational Research* 73: 354–59.

Mann, R.D.; Gibbard, G.S.; and Hartman, J.J. 1967. *Interpersonal Styles and Group Development.* New York: Holt, Rinehart & Winston.

Mann, R.D., et al. 1970. *The College Classroom: Conflict, Change, and Learning.* New York: John Wiley & Sons.

Mark, Michael, and Menson, Betty. June 1982. "Using David Kolb's Experiential Learning Theory in Portfolio Development Courses." In *New Directions for Experiential Learning: Building on Experiences in Adult Development,* edited by Betty Menson. San Francisco: Jossey-Bass.

Marshall, E. Anne. 1985. "Relationship between Client-Learning

Style and Preference for Counselor Approach." *Counselor Education and Supervision* 23: 39–45.

Marton, F.; Hounsell, D.; and Entwistle, N. 1984. *The Experience of Learning*. Edinburgh: Scottish Academic Press. Distributed by Columbia University Press, New York, New York.

Martray, Carl R. 1971. "An Empirical Investigation into the Learning Styles and Retention Patterns of Various Personality Types." Doctoral dissertation, University of Alabama.

Mentkowski, Marcia. 1987. "Assessment/Evaluation: From Data to Decisions." Paper presented at the Fifth Annual Regents' Conference on Higher Education, Nashville, Tennessee, 6 April.

Mentkowski, Marcia, and Strait, M.J. 1983. *A Longitudinal Study of Student Change in Cognitive Development, Learning Styles, and Generic Abilities in an Outcome-Centered Liberal Arts Curriculum.* Report No. 6. Milwaukee: Alverno Productions.

Messick, Samual. 1970. "The Criterion Problem in the Evaluation of Instruction: Assessing Possible, Not Just Intended, Outcomes." In *The Evaluation of Instruction: Issues and Problems*, edited by W.C. Wittrock and David E. Wiley. New York: Holt, Rinehart & Winston.

Milton, O.; Pollio, H.; and Eison, J. 1986. *Making Sense of College Grades*. San Francisco: Jossey-Bass.

Murrell, Patricia H., and Claxton, Charles S. 1987. "Experiential Learning Theory as a Guide for Effective Teaching." *Journal of the Association for Counselor Education and Supervision* 27: 4–14.

Myers, Isabell Briggs. 1976. *Introduction to Type*. Gainesville, Fla.: Center for the Application of Psychological Type.

Myers, Isabell B., and Myers, D.B. 1980. *Gifts Differing*. Palo Alto, Cal.: Consulting Psychologist Press.

National Institute of Education. 1984. *Involvement in Learning: Realizing the Potential of American Higher Education.* Stock No. 065–000–00213–2. Washington, D.C.: U.S. Government Printing Office. ED 246 833. 127 pp. MF–$1.04; PC–$14.01.

Nelson, Karen H. 1975. "Contemporary Models of Cognitive Style: An Introduction." Paper presented at a convention of the American College Personnel Association, March.

Ommen, Jerone L.; Brainard, Stephen R.; and Canfield, Albert A. Spring 1979. "Learning Preferences of Younger and Older Students." *Community College Frontiers* 7: 29–33.

Osipow, S.H.; Carney, C.G.; Winer, J.; Yanico, B.; and Koschier, M. 1980. *Career Decisions Scale.* 2d ed. Columbus, Ohio: Marathon Consulting Press.

Palmer, Parker J. September/October 1987. "Community, Conflict, and Ways of Knowing." *Change* 19: 20–25.

Pask, Gordon. 1975. "Conversational Techniques in the Study and

Practice of Education." *British Journal of Educational Psychology* 46: 12–25.

———. 1976. "Styles and Strategies of Learning." *British Journal of Educational Psychology* 46: 128–48.

Pelsma, Dennis. 1984. "The Effects of Learning Style on Satisfaction with a System of Interactive Guidance and Instruction (SIGI)." Paper presented at the annual convention of the American Association of Counseling and Development, Houston, Texas, March. ED 247 468. 37 pp. MF–$1.04; PC–$5.82.

Pelsma, Dennis M., and Borgers, Sherry B. January 1986. "Experience-Based Ethics: A Developmental Model of Learning Ethical Reasoning." *Journal of Counseling and Development* 64: 311–14.

Perry, William, Jr. 1970. *Intellectual and Ethical Development in the College Years*. New York: Holt, Rinehart & Winston.

———. May 1986. "Review of *The Experience of Learning* [edited by Ference Marton, Dai Hounsell, and Noel Entwistle]." *Harvard Educational Review* 56: 187–94.

Piaget, Jean. 1952. *The Origins of Intelligence in Children*. New York: International University Press.

Pigg, K.E.; Lawrence, B.; and Lacy, W.B. 1980. "Learning Styles in Adult Education: A Study of County Extension Agents." *Adult Education* 30: 233–44.

Ramirez, M., and Castaneda, A. 1974. *Cultural Democracy, Bicognitive Development, and Education*. New York: Academic Press.

Reichmann, S. 1978. "Learning Styles: Their Role in Teaching Evaluation and Course Design." Paper presented at the 86th Annual Meeting of the American Psychological Association, Toronto, Ontario, September. ED 176 136. 15 pp. MF–$1.04; PC–$3.85.

Reichmann, S., and Grasha, A. 1974. "A Rational Approach to Developing and Assessing the Construct Validity of a Student Learning Style Scales Instrument." *Journal of Psychology* 87: 213–23.

Rice, M.A. 1984. "Relationship of Cognitive Style Maps to Achievement and Completion of Educational Telecourses in Community College." Doctoral dissertation, Texas Women's University.

Roberts, D.Y. Spring 1977. "Personalized Learning Processes." *Revista Review Inter-Americana* 7: 139–43.

Roberts, D.Y., and Lee, Hong Yong. December 1977. "Personalizing Learning Processes in Agricultural Economics." *American Journal of Agricultural Economics* 59: 1022–26.

Schmeck, R. 1981. "Improving Learning by Improving Thinking." *Educational Leadership* 38: 384–85.

———. February 1983. "Learning Styles of College Students." In *Individual Differences in Cognition*, edited by R.F. Dillon and R.R. Schmeck. New York: Academic Press.

Siegel, L., and Siegel, L.C. 1965. "Educational Set: A Determinant of Acquisition." *Journal of Educational Psychology* 56: 1–12.

Sims, David, and Ehrhardt, Harryette. March 1978. *Cognitive Style: Utilizing Cognitive Style Mapping in Instruction.* Dallas: Dallas County Community College District.

Smith, Robert M. 1982. *Learning How to Learn: Applied Theory for Adults.* Chicago: Follett Publishing Co.

Stabell, C. 1973. "The Impact of a Conversational Computer System on Human Problem-solving Behavior." Unpublished working paper. Cambridge: Massachusetts Institute of Technology, Sloan School.

Stice, James E. February 1987. "Using Kolb's Learning Cycle to Improve Student Learning." *Engineering Education* 77: 291–96.

Stumpf, Stephen A., and Freedman, Richard D. 1981. "The Learning Style Inventory: Still Less Than Meets the Eye." *Academy of Management Review* 6: 297–99.

Terrell, W.R. October/December 1976. "Anxiety Level Modification by Cognitive Style Matching." *Community/Junior College Research Quarterly* 1: 13–24.

Thomas, Roberta M. March 1986. "Management Team Assessment: A Learning Style Inventory." *Nursing Management:* 39–48.

Toffler, Alvin. 1970. *Future Shock.* New York: Random House.

Torbit, G. 1981. "Counsellor Learning Style: A Variable in Career Choice." *Canadian Counsellor* 15: 193–97.

Vernon, Phillip E. 1973. "Multivariate Approaches to the Study of Cognitive Styles." In *Multivariate Analysis and Psychological Theory*, edited by J.R. Royce. New York: Academic Press.

Witkin, Herman A. 1954. *Personality through Perception: An Experimental and Clinical Study.* Westport, Conn.: Greenwood Press.

———. 1976. "Cognitive Style in Academic Performance and in Teacher-Student Relations." In *Individuality in Learning,* edited by Samual Messick and associates. San Francisco: Jossey-Bass.

INDEX

A

Abstract random style, 34–35
Abstract sequential style, 34
Academic advising, 58–59
"Accommodator" learners, 28, 29, 66
ACT scores, 52, 53
Activists, 67
Adult students, 45, 52
Afro-American culture, 69
Age factor, 45, 52
Allport, Gordon, 3
American College Testing program (see ACT scores)
Analytical learners, 69
Asian students, 70
Assimilator learners, 27, 29, 66
Attitudes
    improved, 54
    toward learning/grading, 43, 45
Attrition (see Dropouts)

B

Bhagavaad Gita, 3
Black students, 69
Body-adjustment test, 8
Business schools, 65

C

Canfield Learning Style Inventory, 51, 52, 53, 59, 60, 63
Canfield model, 51–53, 61
Career choice, 9–10
Career counseling, 61
Career Decision Scale, 60
Chicano students (see Mexican-American Students)
Chinese students, 70
Classroom environment, 40, 78
Cognitive style
    instruction or guidance matching, 11
    mapping, 47–53
Collaborative learning, 12
"College and Career Planning" (course), 50
Communication applications, 58
Comprehension learners, 22
Concrete random style, 34
Concrete sequential style, 34

Conceptual map, 23
Connected vs. separate knowing, 74–75
Converger learners, 27–28, 29
Coping mechanisms, 63
Corby, Jim, 50
Counseling applications, 57–58
Courses
    design, 53
    required, 50, 55
Cultural pluralism, 71
Curricular design, 36–37, 69, 78

D

Deep-elaborative information processing, 24–25
Dental students, 36
Description building, 22–23, 37
Descriptive Test of Language Skills, 60
Developmental theory, 18, 29–30, 63, 67–68
Diverger learners, 27, 29
Dropouts
    analysis, 60, 62
    prediction, 49, 63

E

"Educational set" continuum, 23–24
Edwards Personal Preference Inventory, 14
Eison model, 43, 45, 46
Embedded-figures test, 8, 13
Environmental preferences, 21
Epistemology, 74–76
Ethnic differences, 12–13, 69–71
Euro-American culture, 69
Expectation, 52, 60
Experiential learning model, 25–34, 58
Extroversion-introversion, 14–15

F

Faculty (see also Teaching)
    attitudes toward mapping, 49, 50
    comparison with business managers, 65
    hiring considerations, 78
    instructional design, 32–33
    professional development, 51, 55, 64
    research areas, 54
    type, 15, 16

Field dependence and independence, 8–13
"Field sensitive" concept, 20
Florida State University, 15
Fuhrmann-Jacobs model, 42–46

G

Gestalt approach, 58
"Globetrotting," 23
Grades
    achievement, 49, 54, 59
    expectation, 60
    orientation, 43, 45–46
Grasha-Reichmann model, 40–42
Grasha-Reichmann Student Learning Style Scales (GRSLSS),
    40, 42, 45
Gregorc model, 34–35

H

Hill, Joseph E., 47–51
Hindu theory, 3
Hispanic students (see Mexican-American students)
Holist learning strategy, 21
Holland typology of personality, 19–20, 21

I

Identical-pictures test, 16
"Improvidence," 23
Impulsivity (see Reflection vs. impulsivity)
Individual development
    first attempts to identify differences, 4
    learner/environment interaction, 25–26
    stages, 29–30
Information processing models
    Kolb, 25–34
    overview, 35–38
    Pask research, 21–23
    Schmeck, 24–25
    Siegel and Siegel, 23–24
    student affairs relevance, 57
Institutionalization of innovation, 49–51, 55, 63, 64
Instruction
    design of learning activities, 32
    style, 10–11, 13

Management training, 32
Mann model, 38–40
Mapping, 47–54
Mastery learning concept, 4
Matching and mismatching
      effective learning, 20, 33, 53–55
      instructional/guidance style, 11
      learner/material, 21, 36, 47
      learning improvement, 37
      research questions, 12, 72–73
      student/institution, 35
      student/teacher, 10, 53, 59, 62
      style/developmental stage, 36
Matching-figures test, 16
MBTI (see Myers-Briggs Type Indicator)
Measurement instruments
      body-adjustment, 8
      Canfield Learning Style Inventory, 51
      Career Decision Scale, 60
      Descriptive Test of Language Skills, 60
      Edwards Personal Preference Inventory, 14
      embedded-figures, 8, 13
      Grasha-Reichmann Student Learning Style Scales, 40,
        42, 45
      identical pictures, 16–17
      Kolb Learning Style Inventory, 60, 62, 65
      LOGO, 43
      LOGO II, 43
      matching-figures, 16
      Omnibus Personality Inventory, 18
      Personality Research Form, 61
      Prescription for Learning, 59
      reliability/validity, 72
      rod-and-frame, 8
      Strong-Campbell Interest Inventory, 52, 61
      Survey of Study Habits and Attitudes, 60
      use in work world, 67
Medical students, 47, 62
Mexican American students, 12, 70
Miami-Dade Community College, 52
Miller, Jack, 50
Minority students, 12–13, 69–71
Mode, 52
Models
      Canfield, 51–53, 61
      cognitive style mapping, 47

Dixon, 59
framework, 7–8
Fuhrmann and Jacobs, 42–46
Grasha and Reichmann, 40–42
Gregorc, 34–35
Hill, 47–53, 61
Holland, 19–20
information processing, 21–38
instructional preference, 47–55
Kolb, 25–34, 37, 58, 60, 61
Mann, 38–40
personality, 8–21
Schmeck, 24–25, 57, 63
Siegel and Siegel, 23–24
social interaction, 38–46
Motivation, 45–46
Mountain View Community College, 49, 50, 55
Mt. Hood Community College, 50, 55
Multiple choice tests, 17

N
National Institute of Education: recommendation, 37
Native Americans, 69–70
Nursing, 66

O
O'Mahoney, William, 50
Oakland Community College, 47, 55
Omnibus Personality Inventory (OPI), 18, 20–21
Open-ended tests, 33
Operation learners, 22
Outcomes
    relationship to teaching/learning styles, 23, 42
    research issues, 73

P
Pask, Gordon, 21–23
Peer affiliation, 53
Persistence prediction, 49, 54, 60, 63
Personality models
    field dependence and independence, 8–13
    Holland typology, 19–20
    Myers-Briggs Type Indicator, 13–16
    Omnibus Personality Inventory, 18
    overview, 20–21

reflection vs. impulsivity, 16–17
Personality Research Form, 61
Personality Research Inventory, 14
Personality through Perception, 8
Portfolio development courses, 37
Pragmatists, 67
Prescription for Learning, 59
Problem solving, 66
Procedure building, 22–23, 37
Professional development, 51, 55, 64, 77

Q

Questionnaires (see Measurement instruments)

R

Reading skills, 48, 60
Recruitment device, 62
Reflection vs. impulsivity, 16–17
Reflectors, 67
Relational learners, 69
Research agenda, 78–79
Response styles, 40
Rockland Community College, 59
Rod-and-frame test, 8

S

Schmeck model, 24–25, 57, 63
Self-confidence, 48, 54
Self-esteem, 32, 39
Sensing types, 16
Separate vs. connected knowing, 74–75
Serialist learning strategy, 21–22
Sex differences
    epistemology, 75
    field dependence/independence, 10, 12
    silent students, 40
"Shallow-reiterative" information processing, 24–25
Siegel and Siegel model, 23–24
SIGI (see System of Interactive Guidance and Instruction)
Social-interaction models
    Eison, 43–45
    Fuhrmann-Jacobs, 42–43
    Grasha-Reichmann, 40–43
    Mann, 38–40
    overview, 46

anxiety, 43, 45, 48
construction/objectives, 17, 25, 33
Theorists, 67
Triton College, 52, 53

U

University of California at Berkeley, 18
University of California at San Diego, 42
University of Cincinnati, 40
University of Louisville, 62
University of Michigan, 38
University of South Carolina, 48
University of Texas, 47

V

Values, 60
Verbal behavior, 63
"Versatile learners," 23
Vietnamese students, 70

W

Women's view, 74
Work applications, 65–68

ASHE-ERIC HIGHER EDUCATION REPORTS

Since 1983, the Association for the Study of Higher Education (ASHE) and the ERIC Clearinghouse on Higher Education at the George Washington University have cosponsored the ASHE-ERIC Higher Education Report series. The 1987 series is the sixteenth overall, with the American Association for Higher Education having served as cosponsor before 1983.

Each monograph is the definitive analysis of a tough higher education problem, based on thorough research of pertinent literature and institutional experiences. After topics are identified by a national survey, noted practitioners and scholars write the reports, with experts reviewing each manuscript before publication.

Eight monographs (10 monographs before 1985) in the ASHE-ERIC Higher Education Report series are published each year, available individually or by subscription. Subscription to eight issues is $60 regular; $50 for members of AERA, AAHE, and AIR; $40 for members of ASHE (add $7.50 for postage outside the United States).

Prices for single copies, including 4th class postage and handling, are $10.00 regular and $7.50 for members of AERA, AAHE, AIR, and ASHE ($7.50 regular and $6.00 for members for 1983 and 1984 reports, $6.50 regular and $5.00 for members for reports published before 1983). If faster 1st class postage is desired for U.S. and Canadian orders, add $.75 for each publication ordered; overseas, add $4.50. For VISA and MasterCard payments, include card number, expiration date, and signature. Orders under $25 must be prepaid. Bulk discounts are available on orders of 15 or more reports (not applicable to subscriptions). Order from the Publications Department, ASHE-ERIC Higher Education Reports, the George Washington University, One Dupont Circle, Suite 630, Washington, D.C. 20036-1183, or phone us at 202/296-2597. Write for a publication list of all the Higher Education Reports available.

1987 ASHE-ERIC Higher Education Reports

1. Incentive Early Retirement Programs for Faculty: Innovative Responses to a Changing Environment
   Jay L. Chronister and Thomas R. Kepple, Jr.

2. Working Effectively with Trustees: Building Cooperative Campus Leadership
   Barbara E. Taylor

3. Formal Recognition of Employer-Sponsored Instruction: Conflict and Collegiality in Postsecondary Education
   Nancy S. Nash and Elizabeth M. Hawthorne

4. Learning Styles: Implications for Improving Educational Practices
   Charles S. Claxton and Patricia H. Murrell

5. Higher Education Leadership: Enhancing Skills through Professional Development Programs
   Sharon A. McDade

1986 ASHE-ERIC Higher Education Reports

1. Post-tenure Faculty Evaluation: Threat or Opportunity?
   Christine M. Licata

2. Blue Ribbon Commissions and Higher Education: Changing Academe from

---

Learning Styles

the Outside
Janet R. Johnson and Lawrence R. Marcus

3. Responsive Professional Education: Balancing Outcomes and Opportunities
   Joan S. Stark, Malcolm A. Lowther, and Bonnie M.K. Hagerty

4. Increasing Students' Learning: A Faculty Guide to Reducing Stress among Students
   Neal A. Whitman, David C. Spendlove, and Claire H. Clark

5. Student Financial Aid and Women: Equity Dilemma?
   Mary Moran

6. The Master's Degree: Tradition, Diversity, Innovation
   Judith S. Glazer

7. The College, the Constitution, and the Consumer Student: Implications for Policy and Practice
   Robert M. Hendrickson and Annette Gibbs

8. Selecting College and University Personnel: The Quest and the Questions
   Richard A. Kaplowitz

1985 ASHE-ERIC Higher Education Reports

1. Flexibility in Academic Staffing: Effective Policies and Practices
   Kenneth P. Mortimer, Marque Bagshaw, and Andrew T. Masland

2. Associations in Action: The Washington, D.C., Higher Education Community
   Harland G. Bloland

3. And on the Seventh Day: Faculty Consulting and Supplemental Income
   Carol M. Boyer and Darrell R. Lewis

4. Faculty Research Performance: Lessons from the Sciences and Social Sciences
   John W. Creswell

5. Academic Program Reviews: Institutional Approaches, Expectations, and Controversies
   Clifton F. Conrad and Richard F. Wilson

6. Students in Urban Settings: Achieving the Baccalaureate Degree
   Richard C. Richardson, Jr., and Louis W. Bender

7. Serving More Than Students: A Critical Need for College Student Personnel Services
   Peter H. Garland

8. Faculty Participation in Decision Making: Necessity or Luxury?
   Carol E. Floyd

1984 ASHE-ERIC Higher Education Reports

1. Adult Learning: State Policies and Institutional Practices
   K. Patricia Cross and Anne-Marie McCartan

2. Student Stress: Effects and Solutions
   Neal A. Whitman, David C. Spendlove, and Claire H. Clark

3. Part-time Faculty: Higher Education at a Crossroads
   Judith M. Gappa

4. Sex Discrimination Law in Higher Education: The Lessons of the Past Decade
   J. Ralph Lindgren, Patti T. Ota, Perry A. Zirkel, and Nan Van Gieson

5. Faculty Freedom and Institutional Accountability: Interactions and Conflicts
   Steven G. Olswang and Barbara A. Lee

6. The High-Technology Connection: Academic/Industrial Cooperation for Economic Growth
   Lynn G. Johnson

7. Employee Educational Programs: Implications for Industry and Higher Education
   Suzanne W. Morse

8. Academic Libraries: The Changing Knowledge Centers of Colleges and Universities
   Barbara B. Moran

9. Futures Research and the Strategic Planning Process: Implications for Higher Education
   James L. Morrison, William L. Renfro, and Wayne I. Boucher

10. Faculty Workload: Research, Theory, and Interpretation
    Harold E. Yuker

1983 ASHE-ERIC Higher Education Reports

1. The Path to Excellence: Quality Assurance in Higher Education
   Laurence R. Marcus, Anita O. Leone, and Edward D. Goldberg

2. Faculty Recruitment, Retention, and Fair Employment: Obligations and Opportunities
   John S. Waggaman

3. Meeting the Challenges: Developing Faculty Careers
   Michael C.T. Brookes and Katherine L. German

4. Raising Academic Standards: A Guide to Learning Improvement
   Ruth Talbott Keimig

5. Serving Learners at a Distance: A Guide to Program Practices
   Charles E. Feasley

6. Competence, Admissions, and Articulation: Returning to the Basics in Higher Education
   Jean L. Preer

7. Public Service in Higher Education: Practices and Priorities
   Patricia H. Crosson

8. Academic Employment and Retrenchment: Judicial Review and Administrative Action
   Robert M. Hendrickson and Barbara A. Lee

9. Burnout: The New Academic Disease*
   Winifred Albizu Meléndez and Rafael M. de Guzmán

10. Academic Workplace: New Demands, Heightened Tensions
    Ann E. Austin and Zelda F. Gamson

*Out-of-print. Available through EDRS.

Dear Educator,

I welcome the ASHE-ERIC monograph series. The series is a service to those who need brief but dependable analyses of key issues in higher education.

(Rev.) Theodore M. Hesburgh, C.S.C.
President Emeritus, University of Notre Dame

Order Form

Quantity		Amount

_____ Please enter my subscription to the 1987 ASHE-ERIC Higher Education Reports at $60.00, 25% off the cover price ($40.00 ASHE members). _____

_____ Please enter my subscription to the 1988 Higher Education Reports at $60.00 ($40.00 ASHE members). _____

Outside U.S., add $7.50 for postage per series.

Individual reports are available at the following prices:
1985 and forward, $10.00 each ($7.50 for ASHE members).
1983 and 1984, $7.50 each ($6.00 for ASHE members).
1982 and back, $6.50 each ($5.00 for ASHE members).

Please send me the following reports:

_____ Report No. _____ (_____)
_____ Report No. _____ (_____)
_____ Report No. _____ (_____)

SUBTOTAL: _____
Optional 1st Class Shipping ($.75 per book) _____
TOTAL AMOUNT DUE: _____

NOTE: All prices subject to change.

Name _____

Title _____

Institution _____

Address _____

_____

City _____ State _____ Zip _____

Phone _____

Signature _____

☐ Check enclosed, payable to ASHE.
☐ Please charge my credit card:
    ☐ VISA   ☐ MasterCard (check one)

⬜⬜⬜⬜⬜⬜⬜⬜⬜⬜⬜⬜⬜

Expiration date _____

ASHE ERIC®

Send to: ASHE-ERIC Higher Education Reports
The George Washington University
One Dupont Circle, Suite 630, Dept. G4
Washington, D.C. 20036-1183

NOTES

NOTES